Corporate Acquisitions and Mergers in Hong Kong

Corporate Acquisitions and Mergers in Hong Kong

Third Edition

Virginia Tam

K&L Gates

This book was originally published as a chapter in Corporate Acquisitions and Mergers.

General Editor: Peter Begg

Wolters Kluwer

Published by:
Kluwer Law International B.V.
PO Box 316
2400 AH Alphen aan den Rijn
The Netherlands
E-mail: international-sales@wolterskluwer.com
Website: lrus.wolterskluwer.com

Sold and distributed in North, Central and South America by:
Wolters Kluwer Legal & Regulatory U.S.
7201 McKinney Circle
Frederick, MD 21704
United States of America
Email: customer.service@wolterskluwer.com

Sold and distributed in all other countries by:
Air Business Subscriptions
Rockwood House
Haywards Heath
West Sussex
RH16 3DH
United Kingdom
Email: international-customerservice@wolterskluwer.com

Printed on acid-free paper

ISBN 978-94-035-1351-5

e-Book: ISBN 978-94-035-1382-9
web-PDF: ISBN 978-94-035-1413-0

This title is available on www.kluwerlawonline.com

Printed in the United Kingdom.

K&L GATES

K&L Gates delivers legal services on an integrated and global basis, with more than 2 000 lawyers located in 46 cities across 5 continents. The firm represents a broad array of leading global corporations, capital market participants and ambitious middle-market and emerging growth companies in every major industry. The firm also serves public sector entities, educational institutions, philanthropic organizations and individuals. The firm's lawyers counsel clients on their most sophisticated legal challenges in all areas of corporate and regulatory law as well as litigation.

The firm's multi-office corporate and transactional practice is one of the most substantial in the profession. Each year the firm completes hundreds of mergers and acquisitions (M&A) and public and private debt and equity offerings. Our lawyers in the United States, Europe, the Middle East, Asia, Australia and South America are highly experienced in cross-border mergers and acquisitions, securities, regulatory affairs, tax and financing transactions. Several publications have acknowledged the firm's lawyers as leaders in their fields. K&L Gates has been ranked in the 2018 Chambers and Partners Asia Pacific Guide in Corporate/ M&A in Italy, Poland and United Arab Emirates. 2018 Asia Legal 500 recognized K&L Gates in Corporate/M&A in Hong Kong, China and Taiwan. In the 2018 US News-Best Lawyers 'Best Law Firms' survey, the firm's Corporate practice received National Tier 1 rankings for: Corporate Law, Mergers & Acquisitions Law, Private Funds / Hedge Funds Law, Securities / Capital Markets Law, Securities Regulation, Securitization and Structured Finance Law, Tax Law, Mutual Funds Law, Banking and Finance Law, Derivatives and Futures Law, Financial Services Regulation Law, Venture Capital Law and Trusts & Estates Law. The Legal 500 US ranked the group in the M&A: Middle-Market (USD500 m to USD999 m) category for 2018. Our corporate practice continues to grow in market share and recognition. It is regularly ranked as a top law firm in a variety of league tables published by Bloomberg Global Legal Advisor, Thomson Reuters Legal Advisors and Mergermarket Ltd, among others.

The K&L Gates Hong Kong office was established two decades ago. The office has over thirty legal professionals providing the full range of corporate legal services to clients based in Asia as well as those investing in the region. The office's core practices are corporate and securities, private equity investments, cross-border mergers and acquisitions, intellectual property law, international arbitration and commercial disputes. One of the primary focuses of the Hong Kong office is assisting clients with M&A transactions, particularly those involving China. The office works with clients to facilitate the structuring, financing and successful completion of the full range of acquisitions, divestitures, public offerings, private placements, joint ventures/strategic alliances, re-financings, cross-border transactions and other transactions undertaken by clients.

GRANT THORNTON

Sections Taxation Aspects and Accounting Treatment were written with the support of Grant Thornton Hong Kong Limited. Grant Thornton Hong Kong Limited is a member firm of Grant Thornton International Ltd, one of the world's leading independent assurance, tax and advisory advisers with 50 000 people in over 135 countries. Grant Thornton Hong Kong is an integrated part of Grant Thornton China with a comprehensive network of 24 offices, 260 partners and over 5 500 professionals across China. Its clients include a broad base of over 200 public companies, more than 3 000 state-owned enterprises, private companies and multinational companies.

This publication is for informational purposes and does not contain or convey legal advice. The information herein should not be used or relied upon in regard to any particular facts or circumstances without first consulting a lawyer. Any views or opinions presented in this article are solely those of the authors and do not necessarily represent those of the firm.

Author

Virginia Tam focuses on outbound acquisitions and private equity investments for corporate and financial institution clients in Greater China. A lawyer experienced in U.S. securities laws and Hong Kong Listing Rules, Ms. Tam has worked on a broad range of matters within this practice area, including private and public acquisitions, private investment in publicly-traded equities (PIPEs), pre-IPO investments, joint ventures, capital market exits and privatizations.

Her complete biography can be found on http://www.klgates.com/virginia-tam/

Contents

LOCAL ECONOMIC, POLITICAL AND CULTURAL ASPECTS

Political System

[01] Hong Kong is one of the two special administrative regions of the People's Republic of China (the *PRC* or *China*) established under the PRC constitution. This non-sovereign territory maintains a high degree of autonomy with its own currency, economic and political system. Prior to 1 July 1997, Hong Kong was a colony of the United Kingdom of Great Britain and Northern Ireland (the *United Kingdom*).

[02] The Hong Kong government was established under the Basic Law, a constitutional document enacted by the PRC government in accordance with the Joint Declaration of the Government of the United Kingdom and the Government of the PRC on the Question of Hong Kong. The Hong Kong government reports directly to the Central People's Government of the PRC (the '*PRC government*').The Basic Law guarantees Hong Kong with fifty years of autonomy. It expressly gives the PRC government exclusive power over certain matters in Hong Kong, including foreign affairs, defence and the appointment of main government officials, but vests with the Hong Kong government substantial power over the remaining matters.[1]

[03] The Hong Kong government is headed by the Chief Executive and consists of the executive, legislative and judicial branches. Below is a schematic diagram of the government structure:

[1] Chapter II, the Basic Law.

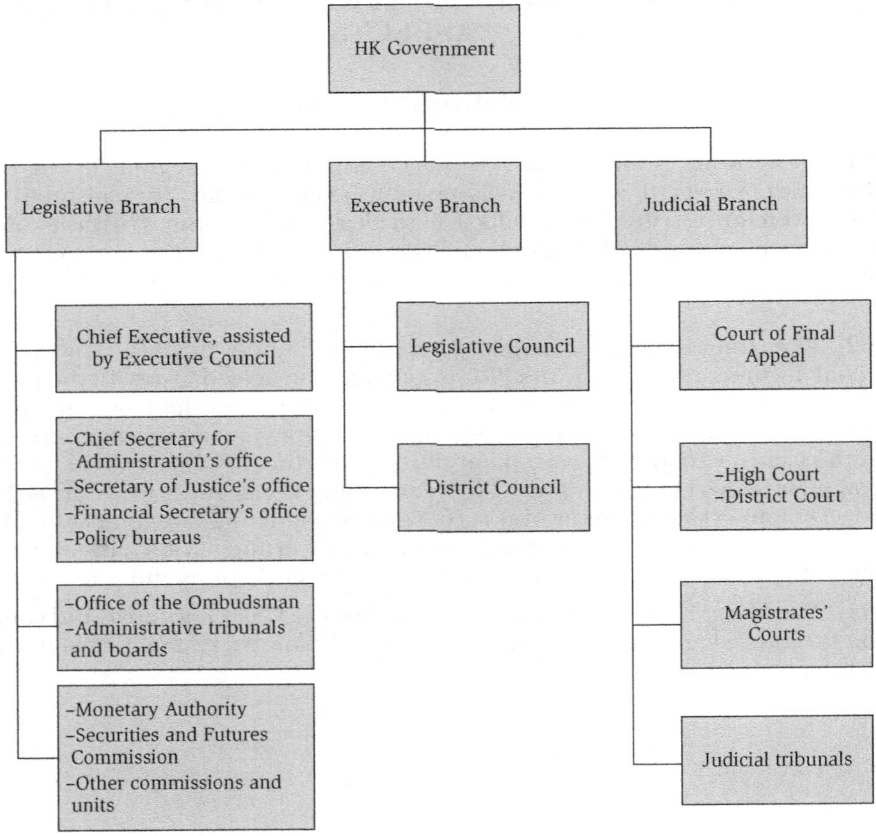

– The executive branch is headed by the Chief Executive, who is assisted by the thirty-two-member Executive Council appointed by the Chief Executive from among senior government officials, members of the Legislative Council and public figures.[2] The current Chief Executive, Ms Lam Cheng Yuet-Ngor, was elected in 2017 with a five-year term by a 1 200-member Election Committee, an electoral college consisting of individuals and entities selected or elected within twenty-eight traditional functional constituencies.[3] The term of all executive council members is for a period no longer than the term of office of the Chief Executive.

The main administration and execution functions of the Hong Kong government are deployed by mostly civil servants in the thirteen policy bureaus and sixty-one departments and agencies.

[2] Article 54, the Basic Law.

[3] Report on the 2017 Chief Executive Election, Electoral Affairs Commission.

– The legislative branch consists of the seventy-member Legislative Council, of which thirty-five members representing geographical constituencies are elected by the general public and the remaining thirty-five members representing twenty-eight traditional functional constituencies are elected largely by 180 000 individuals and entities from select business and professional sectors.[4] Members of the current Legislative Council were elected on 4 September 2016 for a term of four years.

  Members of the Legislative Council are mainly responsible for enacting, amending or repealing laws in accordance with the Basic Law and legal procedures, examining and approving government budgets, approving taxation and public expenditure, and monitoring the work and progress of the Hong Kong government and debating on issues concerning public interests. The Legislative Council also has the authority to endorse the appointment and removal of judges of the Court of Final Appeal and the Chief Judge of the High Court, as well as having the power to impeach the Chief Executive.

  In addition to the Legislative Council, the Hong Kong government is also supported by the District Council comprising of appointed and elected members. All members serve four-year terms. The District Council works on improvement projects and promotes recreational, cultural and community activities. It also advises and liaises with the government on matters that affect the well-being of residents and the adequacy and priorities of government programmes.

– The judicial branch is headed by the Chief Justice, who oversees the operation of courts, magistracies and other judicial bodies. Judges are appointed by the Chief Executive on the recommendation of the Judicial Officers Recommendation Commission, an independent statutory body composed of judges, persons from the legal profession and persons from other sectors. Judges and judicial officers may be recruited from other common law jurisdictions.[5] Under the Basic Law, Hong Kong follows a common law system which was used during its colonial era, and the judiciary continues to be independent of the legislative and executive branches of government, with the power of final adjudication vested in the Court of Final Appeal.

[04] Although the PRC government is responsible for Hong Kong's foreign affairs and defence, Hong Kong is permitted to participate in various international organizations or conferences using the name 'Hong Kong, China', irrespective of whether they are limited to sovereign states, and (subject to the authorization of the PRC government) to enter into international agreements in areas such as aviation and reciprocal judicial assistance, irrespective of whether China is a party.[6]

[05] As stipulated under the Basic Law, Hong Kong's electoral system would be reformed gradually to give the general public more political power in the system. Among others, the original reform timetable was to give the general public the

[4] Legislative Council of Hong Kong, http://www.legco.gov.hk/general/english/intro/about_lc.htm, accessed on 27 Dec. 2018.

[5] Articles 88 and 93, Basic Law and the Judicial Officers Recommendation Commission Ordinance.

[6] Articles 151–153, Basic Law.

power to elect the Chief Executive for the term beginning on 1 July 2017 and thereafter and more power in the election of legislative members for the term beginning on September 2020 and thereafter. The stakeholders could not agree on an electoral reform plan, which resulted in a series of large-scale sit-in street protests, referred to as the Umbrella Movement. The reform plan was indefinitely postponed.

Legal System

Sources of Law

[06] Although the PRC is a civil law jurisdiction, Hong Kong remains a common law jurisdiction with its own independent judicial system. The diagram below summarizes the main sources of Hong Kong law:

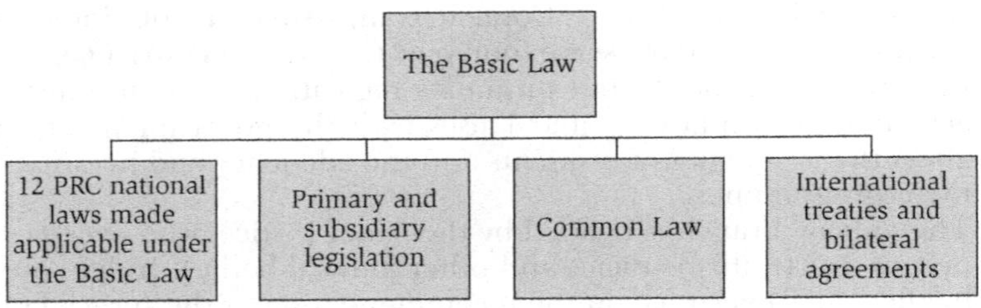

- The Basic Law is the 'mini-constitution' of Hong Kong and the national law of the PRC.
- National laws of the PRC form part of the Hong Kong law if the statute is included in Annex III to the Basic Law. There are currently twelve national laws of the PRC that are specifically made applicable by the Basic Law which are in effect. They include resolutions and laws on the capital, calendar, national anthem, national flag, national day, national emblem, territorial sea and contiguous zone, exclusive economic zone and continental shelf, nationality, garrisoning, diplomatic and consular privileges and immunities and judicial immunity of assets of foreign central banks.[7] The application of a national law in Hong Kong requires either promulgation by the Chief Executive, or by way of local legislation. A national law relating to the national anthem was the national law most recently added to the Basic Law and is undergoing the local legislative process.
- Statutory law consists of statutes enacted by the Legislative Council (referred to locally as *ordinances*) and rules, regulations, bylaws and notices enacted

[7] Article 18 and Annex III, the Basic Law.

under delegated powers (referred to locally as *subsidiary legislation*). References to statutes typically include both the name of the statute and the chapter of the Laws of Hong Kong that it comprises (usually abbreviated to *Cap.*).[8]

- Common law and the rules of equity consist of judgments of the superior courts in Hong Kong and (prior to 1997) of the United Kingdom.[9] Under common law, judges rely on the doctrine of precedent when making court judgments. Article 84 of the Basic Law provides that Hong Kong courts may refer to case precedents from other countries under common law jurisdictions.
- International treaties and agreements form part of the Hong Kong laws if they have been specifically given effect by legislation. Some 200 multilateral treaties currently apply to Hong Kong, although many of them do not apply to the rest of China. For instance, Hong Kong continues to be subject to the International Covenant on Civil and Political Rights.[10]
- Chinese customary law forms part of the Hong Kong law if the practice is currently specifically made relevant by the applicable ordinances.[11]

[07] PRC laws, with the exception of the twelve national laws identified under the Basic Law, are not applicable in Hong Kong. Judgments of mainland courts are not binding on Hong Kong courts.

Enactment of Legislation

[08] Every ordinance of Hong Kong starts out as a 'bill'. The Hong Kong government is responsible for the drafting and introduction of bills. A bill is presented to the Legislative Council after the Chief Executive has consulted the Executive Council. The bill will be published in the Hong Kong Government Gazette and will become an ordinance when it is enacted under the following procedures:[12]

- The first reading is purely formal and is made by the Clerk to the Legislative Council who reads out the title of the bill at a Legislative Council meeting.
- The second reading starts with a speech made by the government official in charge of the bill, who will explain the principles and purpose of the bill. The debate on the bill is usually adjourned, and a committee of the Legislative Council is constituted to consider the merits and principles of the bill in detail. Committee members may make amendments, provided that these are relevant to the subject matter of the bill and do not alter it in principle. When all the clauses have been considered, the chairman of the committee reports to the Legislative Council, and members will debate on the bill and then be asked to vote that the bill be read a second time. If the vote is passed, the bill

[8] Article 8, the Basic Law.

[9] *Ibid.*

[10] Article 39, the Basic Law.

[11] Article 8, the Basic Law.

[12] Passage of a bill, Legislative Council website, http://www.legco.gov.hk/general/english/bills/bill_1216.htm, accessed 27 Dec. 2018.

is given the second reading. If the vote is not passed, the bill cannot proceed further.

- After the second reading, the Legislative Council will go through the clauses of the bill as a 'committee of the whole', making amendments where agreed to. The 'committee of the whole' will then report back to the Legislative Council to consider whether to support the passage of the bill by giving it a third reading. Usually, the resumption of the debate in the second reading and the third reading takes place at the same Legislative Council meeting.
- The bill is then later read formally the third time at the same sitting. A bill that has received its third reading becomes law when it is signed by the Chief Executive and published in the Hong Kong Government Gazette as an ordinance. Unless the ordinance expressly provides for a different effective date, the ordinance becomes effective upon publication.

[09] Newly enacted ordinances are reported to the Standing Committee of the National People's Congress. The National People's Congress is the national legislature of the PRC government, and the Standing Committee is a committee of about 150 members of the National People's Congress charged with exercising the congressional power on a day-to-day basis. The reporting of newly enacted ordinances in Hong Kong to the PRC government is for record only and does not affect their effectiveness. The Standing Committee, however, may return an ordinance on the ground that it is not in conformity with the provisions of the Basic Law.[13]

[10] English and Chinese are the official languages of Hong Kong. Both language texts of an ordinance are presumed to be equally authentic, and the ordinance is to be construed accordingly. This means the Chinese text is neither subordinate to, nor a mere translation of, its English counterpart.

Law Enforcement

[11] The Secretary for Justice has overall responsibility for the conduct of criminal prosecutions and the power to decide whether or not a prosecution should be instituted in any particular case or class of cases. In making that decision, the Secretary for Justice is not subject to any instructions or directions from the Chief Executive. The Secretary for Justice can also initiate civil proceedings on behalf of the government.

[12] Some ordinances vest the power of their enforcement with select government offices, statutory bodies and regulatory agencies. Examples of these include:

- the Independent Commission Against Corruption (against bribery);
- the Equal Opportunities Commission (against discrimination on the grounds of sex, marital status, pregnancy, disability or family status);
- the Companies Registry (against failure to provide statutory information that would result in a compromise of market integrity); and
- the Securities and Futures Commission (against misconduct in the securities and futures markets).

[13] Article 17, the Basic Law.

[13] These government offices, regulatory agencies, and statutory bodies are authorized under the respective ordinances to investigate suspected violation, impose administrative sanctions, initiate civil proceedings and/or cause civil and criminal proceedings to be instituted before judicial bodies. The public may also lodge complaints directly to these agencies and bodies. Their decisions are subject to review by administrative tribunals and courts.

[14] The government may empower multiple enforcement bodies to oversee a specific regulatory area. For instance, the Securities and Futures Commission, the statutory body charged with the regulation of the securities and futures markets in Hong Kong, has the power to bring civil proceedings and minor prosecutions, and to refer market misconduct cases to the Financial Secretary to consider the institution of civil proceedings before the Market Misconduct Tribunal or to the Secretary for Justice to consider the institution of criminal proceedings.

Judicial and Arbitral Proceedings

[15] The power of final adjudication on the laws of Hong Kong is vested with the Court of Final Appeal, the highest appellate court in Hong Kong. Members of the court include the Chief Justice, three permanent judges and thirteen non-permanent judges. Cases are heard by a sitting bench consisting of the Chief Justice, three permanent judges and one non-permanent judge. The powers of the Court of Final Appeal are set out in the Hong Kong Court of Final Appeal Ordinance.

[16] The court hears appeals involving important questions of law, including in particular points of public and constitutional importance, or where leave to appeal has otherwise been granted for some special reason. Although the Court of Final Appeal also has the power to strike down ordinances on the grounds of inconsistency with the Basic Law, the Standing Committee of the National People's Congress has the power to interpret provisions of the Basic Law, and the courts of Hong Kong are bound to follow such interpretations in applying the relevant provision.[14]

[17] Immediately beneath the Court of Final Appeal is the High Court, which consists of two courts:

- The Court of Appeal of the High Court, which hears appeals on civil and criminal matters from the Court of First Instance, the District Courts and the Lands Tribunal. It also makes rulings on questions of law referred to it by the lower courts.
- The Court of First Instance of the High Court, which has unlimited jurisdiction in civil and criminal matters. It also hears appeals from the Magistrates' Courts, the Small Claims Tribunal, the Obscene Articles Tribunal, the Labour Tribunal and the Minor Employment Claims Adjudication Board. The most serious criminal offences are tried by a judge of the Court of First Instance of the High Court sitting with a jury. The court also has jurisdiction

[14] Article 158, the Basic Law.

over admiralty, bankruptcy, company winding-up, family, adoption, probate and mental health matters and hears appeals on points of law involving decisions of the Labour Tribunal and Small Claims Tribunal.

[18] Most criminal cases in Hong Kong are tried by a judge of the District Court or a magistrate of a Magistrate's Court without a jury. The District Court hears all serious cases except murder, manslaughter, rape, armed robbery, trafficking in large quantities of dangerous drugs and complex commercial fraud. The maximum term of imprisonment a District Court judge can impose is seven years.[15] The maximum sentence a magistrate can impose is generally two years' imprisonment for a single offence, and three years' imprisonment where there are two or more indictable offences being dealt with at the same time.[16]

[19] Many civil cases in Hong Kong are tried by a judge of the District Court. The District Court has jurisdiction to hear and determine civil cases where the monetary claims are below HKD3 m[17] or, where the claims are for recovery of land, the annual rent, or rateable value or annual value of the land does not exceed HKD320 000.[18] Those with claims arising from contract or tort that involve amounts not exceeding HKD75 000 come within the jurisdiction of the Small Claims Tribunal.[19] Civil cases where the monetary claims exceed the scope of jurisdiction of the District Court are tried by a judge of the Court of Instance of the High Court. Jury trials are not available for civil cases in Hong Kong.

[20] Some cases are adjudicated before judicial and administrative tribunals set up under specific statutes, such as the following:

- The Labour Tribunal (for specific matters relating to employment).
- The Lands Tribunal (for specific matters relating to construction, occupancy and land use).
- The Obscene Articles Tribunal (for the classification of publications or questions of obscenity or indecency arising in court proceedings).
- The Market Misconduct Tribunal (for specific matters relating to misconduct in the securities markets).

[21] The Hong Kong judiciary has the power to invite judges from other common law jurisdictions to participate in the judicial process, except that the Chief Justice and the Chief Judge of the High Court must be Chinese nationals. The power to recruit foreign judges is derived from the Basic Law. Since the sovereignty transfer in 1997, more local judges have been appointed, resulting in a steady decline in the percentage of foreign judges in the judicial system. A higher proportion of cases are now heard in Chinese.

[22] Arbitration in Hong Kong is governed by the Arbitration Ordinance. The Ordinance is based in part on the UNCITRAL Model Law, the model law drafted

[15] Section 82, District Court Ordinance.
[16] Section 57, Magistrates Ordinance.
[17] Section 32, District Court Ordinance.
[18] Section 35, District Court Ordinance.
[19] Section 5 and Schedule, Small Claims Tribunal Ordinance.

by the United Nations Commission on International Trade Law. The Hong Kong International Arbitration Centre facilitates arbitration in Hong Kong by offering panels of international and local arbitrators and mediators.

Recognition of Judgments and Arbitration Awards

[23] Judgments and awards of the High Court and above may be enforced in most common law jurisdictions and, in consequence of international agreements and arrangements, various foreign countries, including France, Germany and Italy. Reciprocal arrangements exist for the enforcement in Hong Kong of the judgments of the superior courts of those countries that will enforce Hong Kong's judgments.

[24] Arbitration awards made in Hong Kong can be enforced in more than 120 jurisdictions that are signatories to the New York Convention on the Recognition and Enforcement of Foreign Arbitral Awards. Arbitration awards made in mainland China and Hong Kong are also mutually enforceable through a mechanism under the Arbitration Ordinance.

Economic Environment

Economic Indicators

[25] The Hong Kong economy is made competitive by a developed banking sector, a well-regarded legal system, a low incidence of corruption and a simple taxation system. Hong Kong's economy is the 44th biggest economy according to the 2017 World Fact Book published by the Central Intelligence Agency, compared with 15th for South Korea, 23rd for Taiwan and 39th for Singapore. Its gross domestic product (*GDP*) per capita at purchasing power parity is the 17th highest globally in 2017, compared with 19th for the United States, 39th for the United Kingdom and 108th for the PRC.[20]

[26] Hong Kong's legal currency, the Hong Kong dollar, is pegged to the US dollar. Inflation was 1.5% in 2017.[21]

[27] Hong Kong's unemployment rate was 3.1% in 2017.[22] The size of the total labour force in Hong Kong was 3.965 million in 2017.[23] A statutory minimum wage was first introduced in 2011. The general consensus is that the labour market has not been significantly affected by the change.

[20] The World Fact Book https://www.cia.gov/library/publications/the-world-factbook/rankorder/2001 rank.html, accessed 27 Dec. 2018.

[21] *Ibid*.

[22] *Ibid*.

[23] *Ibid*.

Regulatory Climate

[28] The Hong Kong economy is recognized as one of the freest in the world. Historically, the Hong Kong government has adhered to the general principle of positive non-interventionism.

[29] Hong Kong has a simple tax system. The main categories of tax are profits tax, salaries tax and property tax. There is no capital gains tax, withholding tax on dividend or interest income, sales tax, value-added tax, or estate tax in Hong Kong. A major source of the Hong Kong government's revenue is from the sale of leasehold interest in land.

Major Industries

[30] Hong Kong is one of the world's most services-oriented economies, with service sectors accounting for more than 90% of the total GDP in Hong Kong.[24] In terms of GDP generated, the most important service sectors in Hong Kong are trading and logistics, financial services, tourism and professional services. Among others:

- Hong Kong's economy is highly dependent on cross-border corporate finance. The securities exchange operated by the Hong Kong Stock Exchange Limited (the *Stock Exchange* or *Hong Kong Stock Exchange*) is the seventh largest in the world and the third largest in Asia by market capitalization.[25] There were 2 118 companies listed on Hong Kong Stock Exchange and the total market capitalization of Hong Kong's stock market reached USD4.35 trillion in 2017. The Stock Exchange operates two markets: the Main Board and the GEM Board (collectively, the *Hong Kong Stock Market*).
- Hong Kong is an important banking centre in the Asia Pacific. In 2018, there were 187 authorized institutions and 48 representative offices in Hong Kong. According to the Global Financial Centre Index 2018, Hong Kong ranked the third among the leading global financial centres in the world.[26]
- Hong Kong is the world's 7th largest exporter of merchandise trade and 15th largest exporter of commercial services, with mainland China as its most significant trading partner.[27] Hong Kong is one of several hub ports serving Southeast and East Asia and is one of the busiest container ports in the world. There are strong trading links between Hong Kong and the rest of the Asia Pacific region.

[24] Economic and Trade Information published by the Hong Kong Trade Development Council on 28 Nov. 2018.

[25] *Ibid.*

[26] https://www.longfinance.net/programmes/financial-centre-futures/global-financial-centres-index/, accessed 26 Dec. 2018.

[27] Economic and Trade Information published by the Hong Kong Trade Development Council on 28 Nov. 2018.

Relationship with Mainland China

[31] For a long period of time in the territory's history, Hong Kong has functioned mostly as a trading port connecting mainland China with the rest of the world. Following the transfer of sovereignty in 1997 and the rapid economic growth of China in the past two decades, Hong Kong's economic ties with China have become stronger, closer and more complex. The two governments have entered into various bilateral agreements governing their economic, legal and social relationships. Below is a summary of the arrangements between the two governments on trade matters:

- Hong Kong is a separate customs territory from China. It is a full member of the World Trade Organization and does not levy import duties or tariffs.
- The Hong Kong government maintains a series of trade and commerce arrangements with the PRC government under the Closer Economic Partnership Arrangement (*CEPA*). CEPA is a free trade agreement intended to facilitate the trading of goods and services and the joint development of trade and investment between Hong Kong and mainland China. Many types of goods made in Hong Kong enjoy zero import tariff in mainland China under CEPA. Service providers based in Hong Kong enjoy preferential treatment, usually in the form of less stringent ownership and capital restrictions, in various industry sectors in mainland China. Some professional qualifications, most of which related to engineering and financial services, enjoy mutual recognition in both places.
- Hong Kong's financial markets are increasingly integrated with those in mainland China. For the past two decades, Hong Kong has been an important platform for Chinese companies to raise funds in the international capital markets. In November 2014, the Shanghai – Hong Kong Stock Connect was launched to establish mutual stock market access between Hong Kong and mainland China. In August 2016, the Shenzhen – Hong Kong Stock Connect was approved in principle pending the finalization of all necessary regulatory approvals, market readiness and relevant operational arrangements. To further promote the development of bond markets in both Hong Kong and mainland China, the mutual bond market access between Hong Kong and the Chinese mainland (the *Bond Connect*) was launched in 2017. In the same year, the mainland Chinese government officially recognized Hong Kong's role and full participation in the Belt and Road Initiative, a plan on a trans-continental scale targeting to enhance regional cooperation and connectivity involving more than sixty-five countries in Southeast Asia and Europe. As of December 2017, 1 051 mainland companies were listed in Hong Kong with a total market capitalization of USD2.9 trillion and accounted for about 66% of the Stock Exchange's market capitalization.[28]
- Hong Kong is a designated offshore centre for renminbi (*RMB*), China's legal currency. Cross-border RMB businesses, such as the taking of RMB

[28] *Ibid.*

deposits, the offering of RMB-denominated corporate and Chinese government bonds and trade settlements in RMB have been encouraged in recent years through the gradual relaxation of the restrictions against RMB's free flow.

Foreign Investment and Exchange Control

[32] As a general principle, foreign investors in Hong Kong are treated equally with domestic investors, and foreign companies are taxed in the same manner as Hong Kong companies. Other than the traditionally more regulated industries such as broadcasting, there is generally no limitation on foreign ownership of assets in Hong Kong. There are policy exceptions. For instance, the Hong Kong government, in order to discourage speculative real estate purchases in the past few years, imposed an additional 15% stamp duty on the sale of residential properties to non-Hong Kong permanent residents and all corporate buyers. It also significantly increased the ad valorem stamp duty rates for all residential property transactions with the exemption for Hong Kong residents acting on their own behalf and do not own any other residential property in Hong Kong at the time of acquisition of the subject property.[29]

[33] Hong Kong does not impose exchange controls.[30] Similarly, capital movement in Hong Kong is free. There are no restrictions on capital flows into or out of the territory, or remittance of profits or dividends to, foreign investors, although the declaration of dividends of Hong Kong companies must meet certain restrictions under the Companies Ordinance concerning the maintenance of a company's capital.

Cultural Aspects

[34] The vast majority of residents in Hong Kong are Chinese. Because Hong Kong had been a colony of the United Kingdom for around 150 years before sovereignty was transferred back to China, the territory has a separate cultural identity from mainland China and Taiwan. Elements of traditional Chinese values and western values combined have shaped the residents of Hong Kong.

[35] Since the sovereignty transfer in 1997, the government has maintained a 'biliterate and trilingual' policy. Under the policy, Chinese and English are the official written languages, while Cantonese Chinese, English and Mandarin Chinese are Hong Kong's main spoken dialects. In schools, Mandarin Chinese is a core subject, and more and more local schools have chosen to adopt Mandarin Chinese as

[29] The Inland Revenue Department Website, http://www.ird.gov.hk/eng/faq/bsd.htm, accessed 27 Dec. 2018.

[30] www.gov.hk/en/about/abouthk/factsheets/docs/financial_services.pdf.

the medium of instruction in Chinese and Chinese History lessons. Cantonese Chinese remains the local dialect most used by the majority of the residents of Hong Kong in daily life.

[36] Religious freedom is one of the fundamental rights enjoyed by residents in Hong Kong and is protected by the Basic Law and the relevant legislation. A large variety of religious groups are found in Hong Kong, including Buddhism, Taoism, Confucianism, Christianity, Islam, Hinduism, Sikhism and Judaism. Many schools and health and welfare facilities in Hong Kong are operated by religious bodies.

[37] Other than the traditional western holidays such as Christmas and Easter, Hong Kong residents also celebrate traditional Chinese holidays, including the Chinese New Year, which is celebrated during the first day of the Lunar Year; the Dragon Boat Festival, which is celebrated on the fifth day of the fifth lunar month to honour an ancient Chinese poet, Qu Yuan; the Mid-Autumn Festival, which is celebrated on the 15th day of the eighth lunar month where mooncakes, a traditional festival delicacy, are eaten; and the Ching Ming Festival in spring and Chung Yeung Festival in autumn, both of which are marked by visits to ancestral graves.

REGULATORY FRAMEWORK

Overview

Hong Kong Mergers & Acquisitions Transactions

[38] 'Mergers' and 'acquisitions' do not have statutory meanings under Hong Kong law. The term 'mergers and acquisitions' refers generally to corporate transactions that result in a change of control in the target business from the seller to the acquirer. Because there is no simple, court-free amalgamation procedure for the combination of unaffiliated companies under Hong Kong law, acquisition of a target business is generally implemented through the transfer of the target company to the acquirer or by combining the business of the target company with the existing business of the acquirer. These transactions are normally structured in Hong Kong as a stock transfer, an asset sale or a scheme of arrangement.

[39] Hong Kong is a major financial hub for cross-border business transactions and a jurisdiction with an established rule of law. M&A in Hong Kong thus often involve laws of other jurisdictions: Hong Kong businesses can be owned by offshore companies; Hong Kong companies can have substantial offshore operations; shares listed on the Hong Kong Stock market can be issued by offshore companies with offshore assets; and business transactions that do not otherwise have any connections to Hong Kong can be governed by Hong Kong law.

[40] Generally, the Hong Kong regulatory regime is relevant if a transaction involves one or more of the following elements:

- The transaction involves an operator based in Hong Kong (referred to in this article as a '*Hong Kong operator*'), whether the company is the seller, buyer or target; or a company with a large number of Hong Kong shareholders but not listed in Hong Kong (referred to in this article as a 'Hong Kong public company'). Other types of Hong Kong operators are individuals and unincorporated entities such as partnerships. Most of these operators are in the form of corporate entities established under the laws of Hong Kong or an offshore jurisdiction such as the Cayman Islands or the British Virgin Islands. A Hong Kong operator can be a company owned by a small number of shareholders (referred to in this article as a *Hong Kong private company*); a company with securities listed on the Hong Kong Stock Market (referred to in this article as a *Hong Kong listed company* or *listed company*).
- The assets being acquired include business operations in Hong Kong or other assets located in Hong Kong (referred to in this article as *Hong Kong assets*).
- Acquisition financing is sourced from the capital markets, private funds and banks in Hong Kong.
- Some or all of the transaction documents are governed by Hong Kong law.
- A dispute between the parties is resolved in Hong Kong courts or through arbitration in Hong Kong.

The diagram below summarizes the elements normally found existing in a 'Hong Kong Mergers & Acquisitions transaction'.

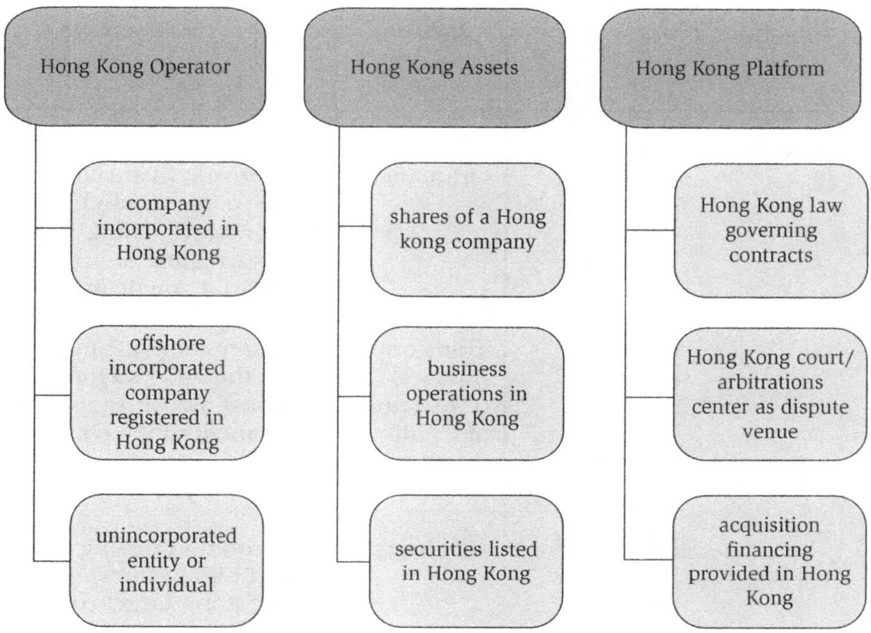

This section will focus on the regulatory framework applicable to mergers & acquisitions transactions involving Hong Kong companies and Hong Kong assets.

Navigating the Hong Kong Regulatory Framework

[41] M&A present a wide range of fact patterns. Each transaction has its unique facts, resulting in numerous permutations of applicable laws, with each applicable law carrying its own qualifications, exceptions and limitations. Our discussion of the laws and regulations here are intended to give readers an overview of the general principles behind the legal framework rather than a technical analysis of the underlying statutory provisions.

[42] The table below summarizes, for the transaction issues indicated, the laws and regulations that may be relevant to a Hong Kong mergers & acquisitions transaction.

Transaction Issues		*Relevant Laws And Regulations*	*Points to Note*
Structuring	Private company	Companies Ordinance	A Hong Kong company may not provide financial assistance to the acquirer purchasing its shares. Hong Kong's merger regime only allows intragroup amalgamation.
		Transfer of Business (Protection of Creditors) Ordinance	Acquirer could assume liability of the seller's Hong Kong business, notwithstanding any agreement to the contrary.
	Listed company	Takeovers Code	An acquirer crossing the 30% shareholding threshold of a Hong Kong target could trigger a mandatory general offer obligation. Privatization requires the approval of a significant percentage of disinterested shareholders.
		Listing Rules	Transactions with a listed company could be lengthy, complex and expensive under the Listing Rules, and a typical process could take six months or more.

Transaction Issues		*Relevant Laws And Regulations*	*Points to Note*
Regulatory approval	Financial services	Banking Ordinance Securities and Futures Ordinance-Insurance Companies Ordinance	Regulatory approval is generally needed for an acquisition of voting power exceeding 10% (or, in some cases, 15%).
	Telecommunications and broadcasting	Telecommunications Ordinance-Broadcasting Ordinance	Certain key licenses have Hong Kong residency requirements. Changes in ownership of license holders are subject to regulatory approval, and competition within the industry will be one of the factors considered.
	Merger between two competitors	Competition Ordinance	The Competition Ordinance prohibits mergers that may substantially reduce competition in Hong Kong. Other than the rules affecting telecommunications and broadcasting companies, there are no across-the-board merger control mechanisms promulgated under this general principle yet.

Transaction Issues		*Relevant Laws And Regulations*	*Points to Note*
Tax	Shares	Stamp Duty Ordinance	In a transfer of Hong Kong shares, an ad valorem stamp duty of 0.2% is levied on the value or consideration of the shares, whichever is higher.
	Real properties	Stamp Duty Ordinance	In a transfer of Hong Kong real property, one or more of the following stamp duties are applicable. – Ad valorem stamp duty, payable on all residential and non-residential properties; assessed based on market value at variable rates; – Special stamp duty, payable on residential properties; assessed based on market value at rates varying from 5% to 20% depending on the period the property was held for; and – Buyer's stamp duty, payable on residential properties; assessed based on market value at a fixed rate of 15% for all buyers other than a Hong Kong permanent resident.
	Business profits	Inland Revenue Ordinance	Hong Kong does not have dividend, capital gain or withholding tax.

Transaction Issues		*Relevant Laws And Regulations*	*Points to Note*
Employment matters	Wages and benefits	Employment Ordinance Minimum Wage Ordinance Mandatory Provident Fund Schemes Ordinance Employees' Compensation Ordinance	There are requirements on minimal wage but not on maximum hours. Although not required by law, many employers in Hong Kong pay an automatic annual bonus of one month's salary at Chinese New Year.
	Termination	Employment Ordinance Anti-discrimination Ordinances Personal Data (Privacy) Ordinance	Terminated employees are eligible to receive severance pay and, in other cases, long service pay. Variation of employment terms could be deemed a constructive termination.

Transaction Issues		*Relevant Laws And Regulations*	*Points to Note*
Environmental matters	Compliance with the law	Air Pollution Control Ordinance Noise Control Ordinance Waste Disposal Ordinance Water Pollution Control Ordinance Dumping at Sea Ordinance Environmental Impact Assessment Ordinance	The Environmental Protection Department has the power to enforce the relevant ordinances. Under the Environmental Impact Assessment Ordinance, developers are required to submit environmental impact assessment reports for the department's approval.
Dispute	Legitimacy of the decision-making process	Common Law Companies Ordinance	Some of the directors' fiduciary duties are codified in the Companies Ordinance, but the fundamental principles are governed by common law.
	Transaction terms	Common Law	Contract law cases in Hong Kong are beginning to show a degree of doctrinal divergence from English law.

Transaction Issues	*Relevant Laws And Regulations*	*Points to Note*
Venue and procedures	High Court Ordinance Arbitration Ordinance Mediation Ordinance	Losing party is liable to pay the litigation costs of the winning party as a general principle. Class actions and contingency fee arrangement are not permitted.

Hong Kong Corporate and Securities Laws

[43] M&A law in Hong Kong consists mainly of the following:

- *Companies Ordinance*. The Companies Ordinance governs the registration of companies incorporated in Hong Kong and non-Hong Kong companies with a place of business in Hong Kong. The ordinance also regulates the affairs of Hong Kong companies, including their internal management, continuing reporting obligations, profit distribution, restructuring and dissolution.

  The Companies Ordinance is administered and enforced by the Companies Registry. The ordinance is reviewed from time to time by the Standing Committee on Company Law Reform, an independent non-statutory body, to ensure that regular amendments are made to meet the needs of the business community and regulators. The existing Companies Ordinance became effective in March 2014.
- *Common Law*. Hong Kong common law principles apply to the fiduciary obligations and other standards of conduct expected of directors and officers of companies incorporated in Hong Kong. The common law of contract and principles of equity apply to the rights, obligations and remedies under sale and purchase agreements that are governed by Hong Kong law. In the context of mergers and acquisitions, common law often runs parallel with statutory law and other regulations. For instance, directors of Hong Kong listed companies are subject to the Listing Rules (as defined below) and the Takeovers Code (as defined below). Although these regulations do not have the force of law, their requirements on Hong Kong listed companies and/or public companies and their controlling persons could have significant impact of the structure, timing and costs of an acquisition.
- *Securities and Futures Ordinance*. The Securities and Futures Ordinance governs the conduct of financial intermediaries, issuers of securities and market operators. In the context of mergers and acquisitions, the following parts of the ordinance are the most relevant:
  (1) Part XV, which requires directors, chief executives and substantial shareholders of Hong Kong listed companies to disclose their voting interests (in some cases subject to a threshold percentage) in such companies.

(2) Part XIVA, which imposes affirmative obligations on Hong Kong listed companies in their handling of material non-public information (referred to locally as *inside information*) in their possession.
(3) Parts XIII and XIV, which impose civil and criminal sanctions on insider dealing and other types of market misconduct.

The Securities and Futures Ordinance is administered and enforced by the Securities and Futures Commission, an independent statutory body responsible for the regulation of securities and futures markets in Hong Kong and the protection of investor interests. The Securities and Futures Commission has the power to license and supervise market participants, such as corporate finance advisors, brokers, automated trading services, investment advisers and fund managers; supervise other market operators, including exchanges and clearing houses; and authorize certain types of investment products, their offering documents and product advertisements for public distribution.

The Market Misconduct Tribunal is an independent quasi-judicial body established under the Securities and Futures Ordinance. This tribunal is set up to help promote market confidence by protecting the interests of the investing public and reducing market malpractice. It is chaired by a judge or former judge of the High Court, and cases are heard before two members. The tribunal has civil jurisdiction over market misconduct cases, such as insider dealing, false trading, price rigging, stock market manipulation, disclosure of information about prohibited transactions and disclosure of false or misleading information inducing transactions in securities and futures contracts.

– *Listing Rules*. Depending on which of the two markets on which the shares are listed, the Rules Governing the Listing of Securities on The Stock Exchange of Hong Kong Limited or the Rules Governing the Listing of Securities on the GEM Board of The Stock Exchange of Hong Kong Limited (collectively, the *Listing Rules*) govern the disclosure, shareholder approval and other regulatory requirements on Hong Kong listed companies.

The Listing Rules are promulgated and administered by the Stock Exchange, a 'recognized exchange company' under the Securities and Futures Ordinance. The Stock Exchange is a wholly owned subsidiary of the Hong Kong Exchanges and Clearing Limited (the *HKEx*), a for-profit corporation whose shares are listed on the Hong Kong Stock Market. The Hong Kong government is the largest shareholder of the HKEx and has the right to appoint six of a maximum of thirteen directors.[31]

The Listing Rules do not have the force of law. They are enforced by the Stock Exchange through the imposition of a wide range of sanctions based on its listing agreements with the companies. The Stock Exchange may impose sanctions upon listed companies and their directors, senior management, substantial shareholders and professional advisers. These sanctions range in severity and include private reprimand, public censure, referral to the Securities and Futures Commission or other relevant regulatory body for

[31] Director's Handbook, September 2018, HKEx.

further investigation, exclusion from the market for a fixed period and, ultimately, suspension or cancellation of a company's listing. The Securities and Futures Commission has the power to oversee the Stock Exchange's performance of its duties.

– *Takeovers Code*. The main purpose of the Codes of Takeovers and Mergers and Share Repurchases (the *Takeovers Code*) is to afford fair treatment to shareholders of public companies affected by acquisitions, mergers and share buy-backs. It applies to all public companies in Hong Kong and those with a primary listing of equity securities in Hong Kong. Whether a Hong Kong public company is a 'public company' for purposes of the Takeovers Code is decided on a case-by-case basis.

The Takeovers Code is administered by the Executive Director of the Corporate Finance Division of the Securities and Futures Commission or any of his delegates (the *Executive*). The Executive has the power to grant waivers in respect of the Takeovers Code requirements. The work of the Executive is overseen by the Takeovers and Mergers Panel (the *Panel*), which hears disciplinary matters in the first instance, reviews rulings by the Executive at the request of any party dissatisfied with such a ruling and considers novel, important or difficult cases referred to it by the Executive. Also involved in the administration of the Takeovers Code is the Appeal Committee, which reviews disciplinary rulings of the Panel for the sole purpose of determining whether any sanction imposed by the Panel is unfair or excessive.

Like the Listing Rules, the Takeovers Code does not have the force of law. It is nonetheless expected to be observed by participants in Hong Kong's financial markets. The Takeovers Code is enforced through sanctions such as public criticism or censure, requiring advisors and other relevant individuals not to act in a given capacity or banning them from appearing before the Executive or the Panel, or the withholding of the facilities of securities markets of Hong Kong.

Leveraging Publicly Available Information

[44] Hong Kong is a reasonably transparent jurisdiction in terms of ownership record. The table below highlights the types of information retrievable from public sources in Hong Kong.

Types of Information	*Sources of Public Record*	*Points to Note*
Corporate		
Basic corporation information of company, such as: – share capital – directors and shareholders – constitutional documents	Companies Registry	Financial information is not publicly available unless the entity is a Hong Kong public company. Voluntary winding-up records for legal entities are available here, not the Official Receiver's Office.
Solvency of company and individuals, such as: – whether an entity was dissolved by voluntary liquidation – pending insolvency proceedings	Official Receiver's Office	For legal entities, a bankruptcy search will show all compulsory company winding-up records (i.e., winding-up order by a court) on the entity. For individuals, a bankruptcy search will show all bankruptcy orders (both undischarged and discharged) on the individual.
Security interest in company assets, such as: – nature of interest – chargee	Companies Registry	Registrable charges only – does not include, for example, fixed charge on shares of subsidiaries.
Registration of business	Inland Revenue Department	If the business is operated by a sole proprietor or partners, details of the individuals are also available.

Types of Information	*Sources of Public Record*	*Points to Note*
Information concerning listed companies: – offering documents – annual and semi-annual reports – trading by major shareholders – material developments	Hong Kong Stock Exchange	Filings made by listed companies are available on the Stock Exchange website. Copies of the relevant contracts are not available online, but most can be obtained from the companies' registered offices for a nominal fee.
Litigation		
Pending litigation and judgments	Courts Judicial tribunals Administrative tribunals and boards Government departments	Searches are typically run through service companies, because the judiciary does not have a centralized database and some proceedings are before tribunals and commissions that do not form part of the judiciary.
Real property		
Title to property, such as: – ownership – third-party security interest – litigation	Land Registry	Hong Kong does not have a registered title system – ownership should be verified by reviewing conveyancing documents. Documents found on the system do not guarantee ownership title or validity of a mortgagee's interest.
Status of property, such as: – plans and permits – illegal structures	Buildings Department	Records for building works and occupation permits.

Types of Information	*Sources of Public Record*	*Points to Note*
Environmental issues	Environmental Protection Department	For large-scale projects, developers are required to commission environmental impact assessment report and obtain government approval.
Personal property		
Intellectual property, such as: – registered patents – trademarks and designs	Intellectual Property Department	Hong Kong does not have a patent grant system – patents are only registrable if they are granted by one of the three designated patent offices: (1) the State Intellectual Property Office in the PRC, (2) the European Patent Office and (3) the United Kingdom Patent Office.Copyrights are not registrable.
Motor vehicles, ships and aircrafts	Transport Department Maritime Department Civil Aviation Department	Separate registration systems are maintained through different departments.

Operation of Hong Kong Businesses

[45] A Hong Kong business may be operated by natural persons, entities and/or natural persons in partnership, or through their ownership in entities with separate legal identities. This section discusses the basic regulatory framework governing different types of business operating vehicles.

The following diagram summarizes the different operating modes available under Hong Kong law.

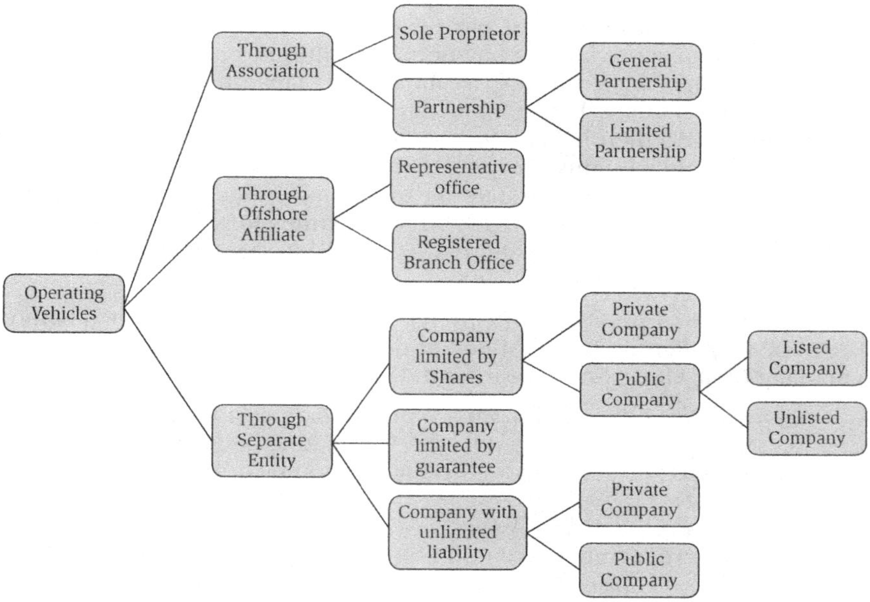

[46] Business operators who choose not to function through a separate legal entity have the following choices:

- *Sole Proprietorship*. Hong Kong businesses may be owned and operated by a single individual. These businesses are operated as sole proprietorships and do not have their own legal identities. Sole proprietors are responsible for all debts and liabilities of their business.
- *General Partnership*. General partnerships established under Hong Kong law are regulated under the Partnership Ordinance. General partnerships do not have a separate legal identity. Partners typically agree on certain terms and conditions of their relations with each other in a partnership agreement. Partnership agreements are not required to be filed with any public registry.

  Every partner in a general partnership under Hong Kong law is jointly liable with the other partners for all debts and obligations of the firm incurred while he or she is a partner, and the firm is liable for loss or injury caused to third parties by wrongful acts or omissions of any partner acting in the ordinary course of the business of the firm or with the authority of his or her fellow partners. Unless otherwise agreed between the partners, general partnerships are dissolved upon the death or bankruptcy of any partner or, in the case of partnerships formed for undefined terms, upon notice by any partner.

- *Limited partnership.* Limited partnerships established under Hong Kong law are governed by the Limited Partnership Ordinance. Like general partnership, limited partnership does not have a separate legal identity under Hong Kong law. Unlike general partnership, however, limited partnership may have one or more limited partners in addition to its general partners. General partners have the responsibility for managing the business and have unlimited liability. Limited partners must not play a part in managing the business, and their liability for the debts and obligations of the partnership is limited to the amount of capital they are required to contribute upon joining the partnership. All limited partnerships operating in Hong Kong are required to be registered with the Companies Registry (if not, the partnership will be treated as a general partnership governed by the Partnership Ordinance by default).

[47] For business operators who prefer to function through an offshore entity instead of a legal entity incorporated under Hong Kong law, they have the option to manage their Hong Kong business in the following manner:

- *Representative Office.* A foreign company may establish a presence in Hong Kong without registering with the Companies Registry if it does not enter into transactions creating legal obligations and confines itself to promotional activities.
- *Registered Branch Office.* A foreign company can conduct business in Hong Kong after registration as a non-Hong Kong company (referred to this article as a *registered branch office*). All dealings with third parties will be made in the name of the foreign company. The foreign company must state on its letterhead and in the places it carries on business in Hong Kong the following information: name, jurisdiction of incorporation and a statement as to whether it is a limited liability company. Registered branch offices are governed by the Companies Ordinance as non-Hong Kong companies.

[48] The following table summarizes the options available to operators who prefer not to incorporate a Hong Kong entity:

	Individual	*Group of Individuals*		*Operating Unit*	
	Sole Proprietorship	*General Partnership*	*Limited Partnership*	*Representative Office*	*Registered Branch Office*
Minimum persons needed	Sole proprietor	Two partners	One general partner and one limited partner	One representative officer	One authorized representative

	Individual	*Group of Individuals*		*Operating Unit*	
	Sole Proprietorship	*General Partnership*	*Limited Partnership*	*Representative Office*	*Registered Branch Office*
Governing documents	None	Partnership Agreement	Limited Partnership Agreement	None	Certificate of Incorporation and articles of association
Advantages	No formalities	Flexible arrangement for business partners	Limited liability for limited partners	Minimal formalities	No need for parent to set up separate legal entity for Hong Kong operations
Disadvantages	Difficult to raise funds and attract talented employees	All partners liable on a joint and several basis	Limited partners cannot participate in operation	Cannot enter into any profit generating activities	Hong Kong operations mingled with offshore operations of parent
Registration with the Inland Revenue Department	Yes, plus annual registration renewal				
Registration with the Companies Registry	No	No	Yes, plus filings for change of particulars	No	Yes, plus filings for change of particulars

	Individual	*Group of Individuals*		*Operating Unit*	
	Sole Proprietorship	*General Partnership*	*Limited Partnership*	*Representative Office*	*Registered Branch Office*
Publicly available information from Companies Registry	-	-	Particulars of partners	-	Particulars of foreign company published in its home jurisdiction; plus charges created on company assets located in Hong Kong
Suitable for	Sole proprietor operating a small, low-risk business	Active business operated jointly by persons with similar status and standing	Standalone project with a limited duration funded by multiple persons	Foreign companies operating a cost centre or conducting testing ground activities	Operators of an active business in Hong Kong that prefer consolidated reporting
Set up time	None	Two weeks	Two weeks	One week	Two weeks

[49] For business operators who prefer to function through legal entities in Hong Kong, most operate through limited liability companies. Unlimited liability companies also exist, but for obvious reasons, few business operators choose this option.

[50] Companies incorporated under Hong Kong law are governed by the Companies Ordinance. The constituent documents of a typical Hong Kong company consist of the certificate of incorporation and the articles of association. Such documents must be filed with the public registry maintained by the Companies Registrar. A Hong Kong company is required to have a registered office in Hong Kong and keep its shareholders registry (locally referred to as the *register of members*) in Hong Kong (although in some circumstances may keep a branch register elsewhere).

[51] There are different types of limited liability companies under Hong Kong law, and they can be classified using the following criteria:

- *Liability of Members.* There are three types: company limited by shares, company limited by guarantee and unlimited company. In the case of a company limited by shares, members' liability for the debts and obligations of the company is limited to the amount of capital that is required to be paid up in respect of their equity interests in the company. In the case of a company limited by guarantee, members' liability for the debts and obligations of the company is limited to the amount they have agreed to contribute to the company in the event of it being wound-up while they are members or generally within a year afterwards.[32] In the case of an unlimited company, members have unlimited liability with respect to the company's debts and obligations.
- *Number of Members.* There are two types: private company and public company. A private company is required to limit the total number of non-employee members to 50 or less, restrict transfers of shares and prohibit invitations to the public to subscribe for its equity or debt securities. Any Hong Kong company that does not satisfy the above requirements is a Hong Kong public company.
- *Trading of Shares.* There are two types: listed company and unlisted company. Shares of a Hong Kong listed company can be traded by the public on one of the two markets operated by the Hong Kong Stock Exchange. Their shares can also be traded in off-market transactions.

[52] The following table summarizes the major types of companies incorporated in Hong Kong.

	Limited by Shares			*Limited by Guarantee*
	Private	*Public*		
		Unlisted	*Listed*	
Minimum persons needed	One company secretary and one director	One company secretary and two directors	One company secretary and at least three independent non-executive directors	One company secretary and one director
Constituent documents	Certificate of Incorporation and articles of association			

[32] Section 170, Companies (Winding-Up and Miscellaneous Provisions) Ordinance.

	Limited by Shares			*Limited by Guarantee*
	Private	*Public*		
		Unlisted	*Listed*	
Advantages	Two tier structure:directors and shareholders	Can have more than 50 shareholders	Shares transferred in a transparent secondary market	No share capital needed; can be public or private companies
Disadvantages	More formalities compared to unincorporated forms	Audited financial information publicly available	High compliance costs	Fundraising using corporate assets could be difficult
Registration with the Inland Revenue Department	Yes, plus annual registration renewal			
Registration with the Companies Registry	Yes, plus filings for change of particulars and annual returns			
Publicly available information from Companies Registry	Particulars of directors, shareholders, company secretary and share capital; plus charges created on company assets	Particulars of directors, shareholders, company secretary and share capital; plus charges created on company assets Audited financial information	All material information about management and business, plus audited financial information, as required by the Listing Rules	Particulars of directors, shareholders, company secretary and share capital; plus charges created on company assets

	Limited by Shares			*Limited by Guarantee*
	Private	*Public*		
		Unlisted	*Listed*	
Suitable for	Operators of an active business in Hong Kong that prefer liability ring-fencing	Companies in need of capital from a large number of shareholders and NGOs	Companies seeking to raise funds from the capital markets	Social enterprises and non-profit organizations
Set up time	Three weeks	Three weeks	Four to six months	Three weeks

FATF Rules in Hong Kong

[53] Hong Kong is a member of the Financial Action Task Force (the *FATF*), an intergovernmental body set up to combat money laundering. Consistent with its obligations as a FATF member, Hong Kong has promulgated anti-money laundering legislation along the lines of recommendations published by the FATF to combat money laundering and terrorist financing. The main legislation consists of the following:

- *Drug Trafficking (Recovery of Proceeds) Ordinance and Organized and Serious Crimes Ordinance*. Under the ordinances, a person commits an offence if he deals with any property, including money, that he knows or has reasonable grounds to believe to represent (directly or indirectly) the proceeds of serious crime (essentially any indictable offence in Hong Kong or any conduct that would be an indictable offence if committed in Hong Kong) or drug trafficking. The ordinances require a report to be made if a person knows or suspects that property represents the proceeds of, or was or is intended to be used in connection with, serious crime[33] or drug trafficking.[34]
- *United Nations (Anti-Terrorism Measures) Ordinance*. The ordinance prohibits a person providing or collecting any property where the person intends or knows that the property will be used to commit terrorist acts[35] (the key terms here are defined broadly) or is terrorist property. It also prohibits a person making property or financial services available to or for the benefit of someone where the person knows that or is reckless as to whether, the other person is a terrorist or a terrorist associate[36] (again, these terms are defined

[33] Section 25, Organized and Serious Crimes Ordinance.

[34] Section 25A, Drug trafficking (Recovery of proceeds) Ordinance.

[35] Section 7, United Nations (Anti-Terrorism Measures) Ordinance.

[36] Section 8, United Nations (Anti-Terrorism Measures) Ordinance.

broadly). The ordinance requires a report to be made if a person knows or suspects that property is terrorist property.[37]

- *Anti-Money Laundering and Counter-Terrorist Financing (Financial Institutions) Ordinance*. The ordinance applies to most types of financial institutions and providers of financial services in Hong Kong, including remittance agents and money-changers. It sets out the standards applicable to these institutions and service providers in terms of customer and transactional due diligence and ongoing relationship monitoring.

Implications on Mergers and Acquisitions

[54] The following summarizes the issues to consider, from a regulatory perspective, when deciding whether to operate a business in Hong Kong:

- Hong Kong is a business-friendly jurisdiction where foreign and local owners can compete largely on an equal regulatory footing. Except for the more sensitive industries, such as broadcasting, a Hong Kong business need not be operated by a Hong Kong company. In finding a suitable operating vehicle for a Hong Kong business, acquirers often find that the answer is driven not so much by Hong Kong law but by the tax law of their home jurisdictions.
- Setting up a 'plain vanilla' business vehicle or registering a foreign business vehicle in Hong Kong is relatively simple and can be completed in as little as ten days. The remittance of funds into Hong Kong is also a relatively speedy process, and settlement can be made in foreign currencies. However, a new bank account could hardly be set up in a day or two in light of the due diligence requirements. Acquirers should, therefore, make advance planning.
- To conduct business through an offshore company in Hong Kong, one should take into account of the FATF Rules and avoid jurisdictions that may flag issues of terrorism or money laundering. Major financial institutions in Hong Kong are often reluctant to enter into business relationships with companies from 'suspect jurisdictions'.

Regulations Applicable to Business Entities

General

[55] As a general principle, all business entities must be registered with the Inland Revenue Department, the Hong Kong tax authority. Exceptions to the general registration requirement are found in some of the more regulated industries. An example is bank representative offices, which are governed and administered by the Hong Kong Monetary Authority and must register under separate ordinances. The requirements and procedures for business registration are governed by the Business Registration Ordinance. As evidence for such registration, each business

[37] Section 12, United Nations (Anti-Terrorism Measures) Ordinance.

operator in Hong Kong must display in its premises a registration certificate issued by the Business Registration Office.[38] The Business Registration Office is an administrative unit of the Inland Revenue Department. Registration must be made within one month of the commencement of business, or, where applicable, simultaneously with an application to incorporate a local company or register a foreign company in Hong Kong.[39] Registration must be renewed annually.

[56] Business registration with the Inland Revenue Department is separate from and in addition to, registration with the Companies Registry (if required). The two registration processes have been streamlined so that a one-stop company and business registration service is available. Under this streamlined process, any person who submits an incorporation form of a Hong Kong company or an application form for registration of a Hong Kong branch at the Companies Registry will be deemed to have made a business registration application with the Inland Revenue Department at the same time.[40]

[57] Apart from the requirements of incorporation or registration of a Hong Kong company or registered branch office and the application for business registration under Hong Kong law, some business activities also require separate licences from other regulatory agencies. Examples of such businesses include employment agencies, travel agencies, restaurants, education institutions, financial services firms, event management companies, retailers and trading companies. Depending on the nature of the activities involved, some business operations require more than one license or permit. For example, in order to operate a restaurant, a general restaurant license is required.[41] If the restaurant wishes to have alfresco dining, an additional license or permit is required.[42]

Private Companies

[58] Most businesses in Hong Kong are operated through Hong Kong private companies. The formation, operation and dissolution of Hong Kong private companies are governed by the Companies Ordinance.

[59] The following sets forth the organization structure of a Hong Kong private company:

- *Constituent Documents.* The constituent documents of the company are its articles of association. Broadly speaking, the articles of association contain regulations for the company's internal management and control.

[38] Section 12, Business Registration Ordinance.

[39] Section 5, Business Registration Ordinance.

[40] Sections 5A and 5B, Business Registration Ordinance.

[41] http://www.fehd.gov.hk/english/licensing/Guide_on_Types_of_Licences_Required.html, accessed on 27 Dec. 2018.

[42] http://www.fehd.gov.hk/english/howtoseries/forms/new/OSA_Guide.pdf, accessed on 27 Dec. 2018.

- *Capital Structure.* There is no minimum level of paid-up capital, although companies engaging in business in certain sectors are subject to specific capital requirements in respect of those activities. The concepts of par value, nominal value or share premium do not apply.[43]

  The share capital of the company can be divided into different classes of shares, such as common shares, preference shares and redeemable shares. Different classes of shares can carry differing rights such as voting rights, dividend rights and liquidation rights.
- *Directors.* The board of directors is the governing body of the company. The company must have at least one director.[44] Corporate directors are permitted, so long as at least one director is a natural person.[45] Directors need not be Hong Kong residents.
- *Members.* The minimum number of shareholders, or members, is one. Members need not reside in Hong Kong and corporate members are permitted. Subsidiaries are generally not permitted to hold shares in their holding entities.[46] Shares may be beneficially owned by someone other than the registered holder.
- *Company Secretary.* The company must have a company secretary responsible for the maintenance of the company's statutory books and records. The company secretary can be an individual or a corporate entity but must be ordinarily resident in Hong Kong. A director may also act as the company secretary but not in circumstances where he is the sole director of the company.[47] Further, where something is required to be done by or to a director and the secretary of a company, one person cannot act in such a dual capacity.[48]

[60] As in many other jurisdictions, a Hong Kong private company is subject to ongoing reporting requirements. The key ones are summarized below:

- *Registered Office.* The company must maintain a registered office in Hong Kong.[49] This need not be the same place as where the company carries on its business. The registered office is the address for service of all official correspondence and any court proceedings. The company's business can be carried on in any part of the world that the management of the company deems appropriate.
- *Annual Return.* Unless in dormant status, the company must file an annual return with the Companies Registry each year.[50] Included in each annual return are various details relating to the company itself: names and addresses

[43] Paragraph 5 of http://www.cr.gov.hk/en/companies_ordinance/docs/briefingnotes_part04-e.pdf, assessed on 27 Dec. 2018.

[44] Section 454, Companies Ordinance.

[45] Section 457, Companies Ordinance.

[46] Section 113, Companies Ordinance.

[47] Section 475, Companies Ordinance.

[48] Section 479, Companies Ordinance.

[49] Section 658(1), Companies Ordinance.

[50] Section 662, Companies Ordinance.

of officers and shareholders of the company, capital structure, debt secured by mortgages and charges that are required to be registered in Hong Kong.[51]

– *Registers*. The company must maintain a register of members in Hong Kong. The company must also keep in Hong Kong a register of charges that contain a short description of each fixed or floating charge given over its assets (irrespective of whether it is registrable). The description should contain the amount secured and the particulars of the assets charged.[52] Charges that are registrable under Hong Kong law include floating charges, charges over land, ships, goodwill, book debts, trademarks, patents and copyrights, aircraft and instalments on the issue price of shares that are due but not paid. From 1 March 2018, all companies incorporated in Hong Kong (except listed companies) are also required to maintain a register of significant controllers. Significant controllers are persons or entities who satisfy one or more of the conditions set out in the Companies (Amendment) Ordinance 2018 (e.g., holding more than 25% of the issued shares or voting rights of the Company directly or indirectly).[53]
– *Changes in Material Particulars*. The company must file with the Companies Registry notice of certain changes in particulars or information previously provided. Changes in any of the following particulars are considered material: directors,[54] secretary,[55] registered office,[56] name of the company,[57] constituent documents,[58] and the particulars of any registrable charge created by the company over its assets or exists in respect of assets acquired by the company.[59] Different filing deadlines apply depending on the nature of the changes. For example, filings in respect of a registrable charge must be made within one month of the creation of the charge or the acquisition of such assets, as the case may be, with slightly more time permitted where the assets in question are outside Hong Kong and the charge was created outside Hong Kong. The Company does not have to file notices in relation to changes with respect to its significant controller. However, it is under a continuing duty to investigate and update its register of significant controllers and to report changes in the location where its register is kept.[60]

Non-Hong Kong Companies

[61] Also known as registered branches, non-Hong Kong companies are foreign companies registered with the Hong Kong Companies Registry. Under Part XVI of

[51] Schedule 6, Part 1, Companies Ordinance.
[52] Section 352, Companies Ordinance.
[53] Section 653E, Companies (Amendment) Ordinance 2018.
[54] Section 645, Companies Ordinance.
[55] Section 652(2), Companies Ordinance.
[56] Section 658(3), Companies Ordinance.
[57] Section 107(2), Companies Ordinance.
[58] Sections 88(5)(a), 89(6)(a) and 90(5)(a), Companies Ordinance.
[59] Section 335, Companies Ordinance.
[60] Section 653P, Companies (Amendment) Ordinance 2018.

the Companies Ordinance, 'a non-Hong Kong company' incorporated outside Hong Kong (referred to in this article as *foreign companies*) with a 'place of business' in Hong Kong is required to register with the Companies Registry. 'Place of business' is broadly defined to include share transfer or share registration offices and places used for the manufacturing or warehousing of goods. Hence, most foreign companies with direct operations in Hong Kong find it necessary to register, unless their operations are confined to non-revenue generating activities, in which case they may operate through a representative office.

[62] The organizational structure of a non-Hong Kong company is prescribed by the laws of its jurisdiction of incorporation. Non-Hong Kong companies are subject to slightly less stringent ongoing reporting requirements compared with Hong Kong private companies. Specifically:

- *Authorized Representative*. A non-Hong Kong company does not have to maintain a registered office in Hong Kong. However, it must appoint an 'authorized representative' to accept on behalf of the company service of process and any notices required to be served on the company in Hong Kong.[61]
- *Changes in Material Particulars*. As in the case of a Hong Kong company, a non-Hong Kong company must file with the Companies Registry changes in certain material particulars. The reportable changes, however, are much more limited and do not include changes in details of various actions and transactions affecting the debt or equity capital of the foreign company and the creation of charges over assets located outside Hong Kong. Specifically, a filing is needed only for changes in the following: constituent documents, directors (and secretary where relevant), authorized representative(s), registered office or principal place of business.[62]

Public Companies

[63] The Companies Ordinance draws an important distinction between private companies and public companies. 'Private companies' must satisfy the following statutory requirements:[63]

- restriction on the right to transfer shares;
- limitation of the number of shareholders to no more than fifty subject to certain exceptions; and
- prohibition of any invitation to the public to subscribe for shares in or debentures of the company.

A Hong Kong company that does not meet the above criteria could be deemed to be a 'public company'.

[64] The Companies Ordinance imposes more stringent requirements on the organization structure and ongoing compliance of a Hong Kong public company.

[61] Section 786, Companies Ordinance.

[62] Section 791, Companies Ordinance.

[63] Section 11, Companies Ordinance.

For instance, the company must have at least two directors instead of one,[64] and corporate directors are not permitted.[65] The company must file its financial statements and its auditors' and directors' reports, as a matter of public record, with the Companies Registry.

[65] Unlisted Hong Kong public companies are relatively rare. They are usually companies that have a large number of shareholders due to their fundraising history or non-profit organizations that favour increased transparency for policy reasons.

Listed Companies

[66] All companies with shares that can be publicly traded in Hong Kong are listed on either the Main Board or the GEM Board, and these companies can be listed concurrently in other offshore securities exchanges as well. The Main Board and GEM Board are regulated and operated by the Hong Kong Stock Exchange. The two trading markets target different types of issuers and have similar but different listing requirements. For convenience, our reference to a Hong Kong listed company is to a company with equity securities listed on the Main Board.

[67] The following sets forth the organization of a Hong Kong listed company and the required corporate governance standards:

- *Jurisdiction of Incorporation*. The company does not have to be a company incorporated in Hong Kong, but the Stock Exchange has the right to refuse to list a company incorporated in another jurisdiction if it is not satisfied that the foreign jurisdiction has standards of shareholder protection at least equivalent to those in Hong Kong.[66] A substantial majority of companies listed on the Hong Kong Stock Market are Hong Kong, Bermuda or Cayman Islands companies or PRC joint stock limited companies. As at 28 November 2018, the Stock Exchange has formally ruled twenty-eight jurisdictions to be acceptable as an issuer's place of incorporation, including the states of California and Delaware of the United States, the provinces of Alberta, British Columbia and Ontario in Canada, the Republic of Korea, Labuan, Russia, and, recently, Israel.[67]
- *Corporate Governance Standards*. The corporate governance standards applicable to a Hong Kong listed company can be classified into three types: (a) standards set forth in the main chapters of the Listing Rules, which are mandatory; (b) provisions labelled as 'code provisions' in the Corporate Governance Code, which are optional but the non-compliance of which must be

[64] Section 453, Companies Ordinance.

[65] Section 456, Companies Ordinance.

[66] Main Board Listing Rules 19.05.

[67] https://www.hkex.com.hk/Listing/Rules-and-Guidance/Other-Resources/Listing-of-Overseas-Companies/List-of-Acceptable-Overseas-Jurisdictions?sc_lang=en, accessed on 26 Dec. 2018.

disclosed and explained in interim reports and annual reports; and (c) provisions labelled as 'recommended best practices' in the Corporate Governance Code, which are encouraged but not required and the non-compliance of which need not be disclosed. For recommended best practices, issuers may devise their own protocols on terms they consider appropriate.

In addition to the disclosure requirement under the Corporate Governance Code, a Hong Kong listed company must include a Corporate Governance Report prepared by the board of directors in annual reports and must contain all required information set out in Appendix 14 of the Listing Rules. Any failure to make such disclosure is a breach of the Listing Rules.

- *Board of Directors*. A Hong Kong listed company must have at least three independent non-executive directors, and independent non-executive directors must represent at least one-third of the board with at least one independent non-executive director having the appropriate professional qualifications or accounting or relating financial management expertise.[68]

  Board meetings must be held at least four times a year, and the chairman has to hold meetings with the non-executive directors at least once a year without the executive directors present. The Corporate Governance Code also requires directors to participate in continuous professional development to develop and refresh their knowledge and skills and the company to arrange and fund suitable training for its directors, with an appropriate emphasis on the roles, functions and duties of a listed company director. Although the Stock Exchange does not specify the amount of training a director should complete per year, directors are required to provide a record of training they have received to the company. Further, to enable the board as a whole and each director to discharge their duties, the management of a listed company must provide all of its directors with monthly updates on company performance, position and prospects in sufficient detail.
- *Chairman of the Board*. The Corporate Governance Code recommends (but does not require) a clear division between the responsibilities of the board and the day-to-day management of the company's business. Thus the roles of chairman and chief executive officer should be separate and should not be performed by the same individual.
- *Audit, Remuneration and Nomination Committees*. The company must establish an audit committee chaired by an independent non-executive director and consisting of a majority of the independent non-executive directors its terms of reference approved by the board. The minimum number of committee members is three, and at least one member must be an independent non-executive director with the appropriate professional qualifications or related financial management experience.[69] A company must disclose immediately any non-compliance of the above requirements by an announcement and meet the requirements within three months after failing to meet them.[70]

[68] Main Board Listing Rules 3.10 and 3.10A.
[69] Main Board Listing Rules 3.21 and 3.22.
[70] Main Board Listing Rule 3.23.

The company must also establish a remuneration committee chaired by an independent non-executive director and consisting of a majority of the independent non-executive directors with its terms of reference approved by the board.[71] A company must disclose immediately any non-compliance of the above requirements by an announcement and meet the requirements within three months after failing to meet them.[72]

The Corporate Governance Code recommends (but does not require) the establishment of a nomination committee consisting of a majority of the independent non-executive directors with specific terms of reference. The nomination committee should be chaired by the chairman of the board or an independent non-executive director.

- *Company Secretary*. The company must have a company secretary who is a natural person with either the required academic or professional qualifications (e.g., being a member of the Hong Kong Institute of Chartered Secretaries) or the relevant experience.[73] The company secretary is required to take no less than fifteen hours of relevant professional training in each financial year[74] but need not be ordinarily resident in Hong Kong. The Corporate Governance Code recommends (but does not require) that the company secretary report directly to the chairman or the chief executive.
- *Public Float*. At least 25% of the company's total issued share capital must at all times be held by the public, although the Stock Exchange may accept a lower percentage of between 15% and 25% for companies with a large market capitalization. The Stock Exchange may suspend trading of the company if the public float requirement is not met.[75]

[68] A Hong Kong listed company must comply with the following disclosure requirements:

- *General Principles*. The company must treat all holders of its securities fairly and equally, issue and market securities in a fair and orderly manner and ensure that sufficient information is disclosed to potential investors.[76]
- *Periodic Reports*. The company must send to all its shareholders its annual report not less than twenty-one days before its annual shareholders' meeting or not later than four months after its financial year end, whichever is earlier, and its semi-annual report not less than three months after the end of the interim period. It must also issue, at a minimum, full-year financial results and semi-annual financial results by way of an announcement no later than thirty minutes before trading on the day after the financial results are approved by the board. Included in such annual and interim reports are accounts of the company, which must be prepared in accordance with the Hong Kong Financial Reporting Standards (*HKFRS*) or the International

[71] Main Board Listing Rules 3.25 and 3.26.

[72] Main Board Listing Rule 3.27.

[73] Main Board Listing Rule 3.28.

[74] Main Board Listing Rule 3.29.

[75] Main Board Listing Rule 8.08.

[76] Main Board Listing Rules 2.03(2) and 2.03(4).

Financial Reporting Standards (other than PRC companies or bank companies, which have their respective standards).[77]

- *Disclosure on Corporate Governance Matters*. The company must disclose in its periodic reports whether it has complied with the provisions under the Corporate Governance Code and the reasons for any deviations and specific information on corporate governance matters, such as the attendance of each director at board and general meetings, corporate governance policy and duties performed by the board and the board committees, and procedures for shareholders to put forward proposals in shareholders' meetings.[78]

  In addition to the periodic disclosure described above, the company must publish an announcement as soon as practicable following certain changes in its organizational structure or corporate governance matters, including the following:
  (1) any changes in directorship, supervisor or chief executive (including appointment, resignation, re-designation, retirement or removal) and any changes in the holding of an executive office, including changes in any important function or executive responsibilities of a director;
  (2) any changes in its auditors or financial year end;
  (3) a director becomes the subject of bankruptcy or related proceedings or some other investigation or criminal proceedings; and
  (4) a decision is reached by the board to change the company secretary, share registrar, registered address or agent for the service of process or the company's name.
- *Environmental, Social and Governance Reports*. The company must publish under the Environmental, Social and Governance Reporting Guide, once a year, an environmental, social and governance report in its annual. The report must comply with the requirements which cover three areas under 'Environmental' and eight areas under 'Social'. Each covered area requires general disclosures on a 'Comply or Explain' basis with reference to the company's policies and some also require disclosure on compliance with the relevant laws and regulations that have a significant impact on the company should be made.
- *Disclosure of Material Developments*. The company must immediately publish an announcement upon the occurrence of certain events relevant to the company's business, including the following:
  (1) receipt or making of a takeover offer;
  (2) entering into a non-exempt 'connected transaction';
  (3) entering into a 'notifiable transaction';
  (4) pledging of shares by the controlling shareholder to secure obligations of the company or entering into a loan agreement with covenants relating to specific performance of the controlling shareholder or breach of the terms of a significant loan;

[77] Main Board Listing Rule Appendix 16.

[78] Main Board Listing Rule 13.89 and Appendix 14.

(5) proposal to issue convertible securities, warrants and options, to issue bonus shares, to make a rights issue or open offer;
(6) material matters that impact on profit forecasts; and
(7) winding-up and liquidations.

– *General Disclosure and Simultaneous Trading Halt Obligation*. The company must publish an announcement and apply for a trading halt as soon as reasonably practicable if the company becomes aware of information (including information on any major new development in its sphere of activity that is not public knowledge) that:
(1) is necessary to enable them and the public to appraise the position of the company;
(2) is necessary to avoid the establishment of a false market in its securities; or
(3) is reasonably expected to materially affect market activity in and the price of its securities.

Matters such as unusual trading volume and price movement of shares, complaints received by or regarding the company, and the entering into a non-binding memorandum of understanding on proposed transactions may give rise to this disclosure and trading halt obligation. It is for the company to make the assessment and judgment on whether the matter at hand may cause a false market if not disclosed. This disclosure obligation exists irrespective of whether the Stock Exchange makes enquiries.

– *Prompt Disclosure of Inside Information*. Under the Securities and Futures Ordinance, the company must disclose 'inside information' to the public as soon as reasonably practicable[79] unless the information falls within any of the safe harbours as provided in the Securities and Futures Ordinance (such as information constituting an incomplete proposal or negotiation).[80] Before the information is fully disclosed to the public, the company must ensure that the information is kept strictly confidential.[81]

To fall within the definition of 'inside information':[82]
(1) the information about the particular company must be specific;
(2) the information must not be generally known to that segment of the market that deals or which would likely deal in the company's securities; and
(3) the information would, if so known, be likely to have a material effect on the price of the company's securities.

The obligation to disclose inside information under the Securities and Futures Ordinance is separate and distinct from the disclosure requirements under the Listing Rules and those under the Takeovers Code.

[79] Section 307B, Securities and Futures Ordinance.
[80] Sections 307B and 307D, Securities and Futures Ordinance.
[81] Section 307D, Securities and Futures Ordinance.
[82] Section 245, Securities and Futures Ordinance.

Implications on Mergers and Acquisitions

[69] The following summarizes the issues to consider when deciding whether to set up a Hong Kong company for an acquisition, re-domicile a Hong Kong business after an acquisition or acquire a Hong Kong listed company:

- Hong Kong company law is well established and benefits from a large body of relevant case law, an independent judiciary and a large pool of practising lawyers. The jurisdiction is also well regarded by other developed countries in terms of its policy against money laundering, terrorism and tax avoidance schemes. However, some find the regime burdensome and inflexible in some areas, such as the lack of a statutory merger regime between unaffiliated Hong Kong companies, the lengthy liquidation process, restrictions against share capital reduction and leveraged buyouts and audited financial statements requirements.
- Many companies operating in Hong Kong, including listed companies, are incorporated offshore. Some of these companies are incorporated in the Cayman Islands, the British Virgin Islands, Bermuda and Jersey, often chosen by their owners with the belief that other jurisdictions could afford shareholders additional privacy and flexibility. Some of these companies are operated as branch offices of foreign companies incorporated in their home jurisdictions, such as Germany, Australia and Canada. In these cases, their owners' decisions are often tax driven or motivated by administrative efficiency.
- The Hong Kong Stock Exchange is an internationally recognized securities exchange. Many Hong Kong listed companies have all or substantially all of their business operations outside Hong Kong. Hong Kong may or may not be the most suitable listing venue for a particular business. Generally, manufacturers, retailers and commercial service providers are more inclined towards listing in Hong Kong because their brands are well-known here. In contrast, telecommunications, media and technology companies are more inclined towards listing in the United States because more stock analysts cover the telecommunications, media and technology sector there. The Hong Kong Stock Exchange is keen to maintain a diversified portfolio of listed companies and has policies accommodating their special needs. For example, listing applicants in the biotechnology and mining sectors and large technology companies benefit from exceptions to some Listing Rules.

Regulations Applicable to Transactions

General

[70] If the target asset is located in Hong Kong or the purchase of the asset is governed by Hong Kong law, the acquirer should ensure that, under Hong Kong law: (a) the asset is transferable, (b) the transfer of the asset will not trigger default in other assets to be acquired in the acquisition (e.g., supplier contract) and (c) all transfer taxes and expenses are budgeted and allocated between the parties in advance. As in many other jurisdictions, acquisition of a Hong Kong target can be accomplished in two ways:

– *Stock Transaction.* A stock transaction involves the purchase of shares in the target company, resulting in the acquirer obtaining all the assets and assuming all the liabilities, of the underlying business. Generally, a stock transaction is simpler to execute compared with an asset transaction, but the level of due diligence required is substantially similar, if not more.
– *Asset Transaction.* An asset transaction involves the purchase of assets of the target company, resulting in the acquirer obtaining ownership of selected assets but not, in some cases, assuming the liabilities of the underlying business. These assets include not only tangible properties such as real properties, machinery and inventories but also intangible ones such as the target company's interests in its shares of subsidiaries, permits and licences, intellectual properties and contracts.

[71] The following diagram summarizes the issues commonly encountered in a typical acquisition:

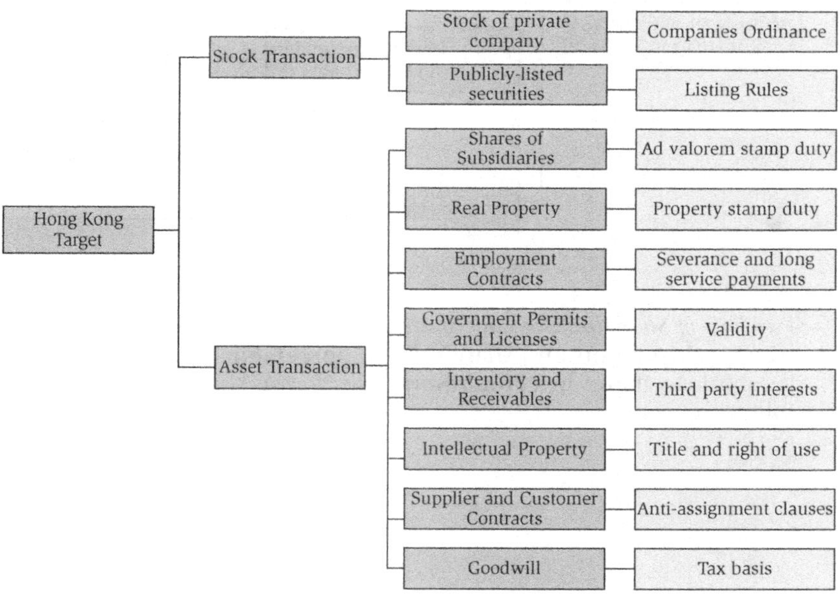

Acquisition of Hong Kong Shares

[72] The acquisition of shares in a Hong Kong private company is relatively straightforward from a regulatory standpoint. In most cases, complete or partial transfer of ownership of the target company is achieved with limited Hong Kong regulatory and statutory constraints. The transfer of shares of a non-Hong Kong company is not subject to the processes described below. However, if the non-Hong Kong company maintains a register of shareholders in Hong Kong, the shares will be deemed to be 'Hong Kong shares' under the Stamp Duty Ordinance, and the transfer of these shares will be subject to the payment of stamp duty.

[73] The acquirer, as the transferee of the target shares, inherits all of the liabilities, including undisclosed or contingent liabilities, of the target company. Liability risk is managed through due diligence on the target company and contractual protections, such as indemnifications and extensive representations and warranties in the sale and purchase agreement.

[74] The following sets forth the options available when acquiring a Hong Kong private company through the purchase of shares:

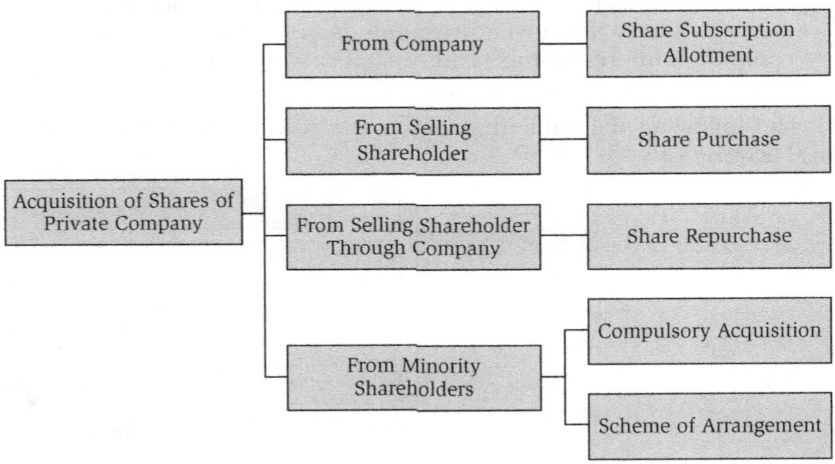

- *Purchase of Shares from Selling Shareholder.* Subject to the target company's constituent documents and shareholders' agreement (if any), the transfer of the legal title to shares in a Hong Kong private company generally consists of the following steps:

Execution of transfer documents	– If there is a transfer of the beneficial ownership of the shares, the parties execute an instrument of transfer and/or related contract notes (referred to locally as *bought note* and *sold note*) under Hong Kong law. – When there is a sale of beneficial ownership without the transfer of legal title (such as a transfer of ownership interest at the corporate shareholder level), an instrument of transfer is not required. – When there is a divergence between the beneficial and legal interests, it would be in the interest of the beneficial owner and the legal title owner to execute a declaration of trust. However, under the Companies Ordinance, no notice of any trust, whether expressed, implied or constructive, can be entered on the register of members.
Payment of Stamp Duty	– The parties submit the instrument of transfer and/or related contract notes to the Stamp Office, a division of the Inland Revenue Department, for stamping, along with payment of the required stamp duty, within 2 days (or 30 days if the sale takes place outside Hong Kong) of their execution. – The submission is accompanied by: (i) a copy of the latest audited accounts or latest management accounts (if audited accounts have not been prepared or if they are not up to date) of the target company, (ii) details of any land and properties held by the company and (iii) a copy of any sale and purchase agreement to the Stamp Office. The Stamp Office may also require additional information. – The payment of stamp duty is exempted under certain circumstances, such as intragroup transfers.
Registration	– After stamping, the transferee can be registered as a shareholder in the statutory books of the company and a new share certificate can be issued.

Statutory Filing	– It is not necessary to report the details of a share transfer to the Companies Registry immediately. The transfer of shares should be reported in the target company's next annual return on Form NAR1.

– *Allotment of Shares by the Company*. The issuance (referred to locally as an *allotment*) of new shares by the target company is governed by the Companies Ordinance, constituent documents of the company and shareholders' agreement (if any). Generally, share allotment consists of the following steps:

Shareholder Approval of the Allotment	– Directors of the target company may only exercise power to allot shares to the acquirer following the receipt of shareholder approval. This approval may be given either in relation to a particular allotment or pursuant to a general mandate granted to the directors in a general meeting. All shareholders of the target company have a statutory pre-emptive right to subscribe shares of the Company. Thus each shareholder must have granted a waiver specific to the allotment or a general waiver.
Application for Shares	– As a matter of corporate records, the acquirer submits a signed application form, setting forth the number of shares subscribed and the subscription price.
Registration	– Hong Kong no longer imposes capital duty on the allotment of shares. Hence the subscriber can be registered as a shareholder in the statutory books of the company immediately after the allotment, and a new share certificate can be issued.
Statutory Filing	– The company submits a return of allotments on Form NSC1 to the Companies Registry within one month after the first day of allotment. If the allotment of shares is made either fully or partly for a consideration otherwise than in cash, the Form NSC1 should be submitted together with the relevant documents.

– *Repurchase of Shares by the Company.* If the acquirer is already an existing shareholder of the target company, it may be possible to structure the acquisition of the remaining shares in the target company as a share repurchase by the target company from the selling shareholder. Compared to a purchase by the acquirer, a repurchase by the target company would enable the direct use of cash assets in the company for the acquisition. For acquirers that are subject to dividend income in their home jurisdiction, this is also a more tax advantageous way for the acquirer to realize the cash assets of the company.

This structure, however, is more difficult to implement due to the general statutory prohibition against share repurchases and the provision of financial assistance by a Hong Kong company for the purchase of its own shares. The relevant restrictions are contained in the Companies Ordinance and include the following:

(1) A Hong Kong company must not buy back its own shares unless the funds are derived out of distributable profits, out of the proceeds of a fresh issue of shares, or out of capital.[83]

(2) A Hong Kong company must not provide financial assistance to a potential acquirer of the company's shares, unless:

(a) the company satisfies the solvency test, which requires that: (i) immediately after the transaction there will be no ground on which the company could be found to be unable to pay its debts; and (ii) either: (x) the company will be able to pay its debts as they become due during the period of twelve months immediately following the transaction, or (y) if the company is intended to commence the winding-up of the company within twelve months after the date of the transaction, the company will be able to pay its debts in full within twelve months after the commencement of its winding-up;[84] and

(b) at least one of the following is satisfied: (i) all other financial assistance previously given and not repaid is in aggregate less than 5% of shareholders' funds;[85] (ii) all shareholders of the company approve the financial assistance by way of a written resolution;[86] or (iii) an ordinary resolution of the company is passed to approve the financial assistance and the assistance is provided within twenty-eight days thereafter.[87]

[83] Section 257, Companies Ordinance.

[84] Section 205, Companies Ordinance.

[85] Section 283, Companies Ordinance.

[86] Section 284, Companies Ordinance.

[87] Section 285, Companies Ordinance.

The following summarizes the procedures required for a share repurchase:

Directors' Solvency Statement	– The directors of the company must make and sign a solvency statement to the effect that the directors have formed the opinion that the company satisfies the solvency test. Each director must enquire into the company's state of affairs and prospects and take into account all liabilities (including contingent and prospective) of the company in forming his opinion.
Approval of Shareholders	– The repurchase contract is approved by a special resolution of disinterested shareholders.
Registration and Statutory Filing	– A share repurchase is treated as a transfer of shares from the remaining shareholders to the target company and is subject to the payment of stamp duty. The other procedures described in 'Purchase of Shares from Selling Shareholder' in this section apply.

– *Compulsory Acquisition (or Squeeze Out).* As in many other jurisdictions, the Companies Ordinance contains a mechanism under which an acquirer can compel minority shareholders to sell the shares (or shares of a particular class) in the target Hong Kong company to the acquirer. To exercise the right of compulsory acquisition (also referred to as *squeeze out*), the acquirer must have successfully completed a 'takeover offer' for the shares (or the shares of the relevant class, as the case may be) in the following manner:
  (1) the acquirer offers to purchase all the shares except those that, at the date of the offer, are held by the acquirer;
  (2) the terms of the takeover offer are the same in relation to all the shares to which the offer relates;[88] and
  (3) acceptances of the takeover offer resulting in the acquirer owning at least 90% in number of the shares of any class to which the offer relates; or if the acquirer could not meet the threshold due to failure to trace one or more shareholders after reasonable enquiry (assuming that these

[88] Section 689, Companies Ordinance.

untraceable shareholders accept the offer), it may apply to the court for authorization to give notices to these untraceable shareholders.[89]

The following summarizes the procedures for a compulsory acquisition under the Companies Ordinance:

Successful Completion of the Takeover Offer	– The acquirer successfully completes the required takeover offer as stipulated above.
Notice to Remaining Shareholders	– The offeror gives notice to non-accepting shareholders before (i) the end of three months after the expiration of the offer period, or (ii) the end of six months after the launch of the offer, whichever is earlier.[90]
Completion of the Compulsory Acquisition	– A non-accepting shareholder may, within two months after the date of the prescribed notice, apply to court objecting to the compulsory purchase. – If there is no such application, or if the court allows the acquirer to proceed with the compulsory purchase, the acquirer, within two months after the date of the prescribed notice, (i) sends to the target company a copy of the notice together with an instrument of transfer executed on behalf of the shareholder (to whom the notice was sent) by a person appointed by the acquirer; and (ii) pays the relevant consideration.[91]

- *Scheme of Arrangement*. If the acquirer is already a shareholder of the target company, the acquirer may file an application proposing a rearrangement between the target company and its shareholders.[92] The court will review the proposed rearrangement (known as a *scheme*) for fairness and, if so, order a meeting to be held of the shareholders affected. The court has discretion to group shareholders into separate classes on the basis of commonality of right.

[89] Section 693, Companies Ordinance.
[90] Section 694, Companies Ordinance.
[91] Section 696, Companies Ordinance.
[92] Section 670, Companies Ordinance.

The following summarizes the procedures required for a scheme of arrangement initiated by an existing shareholder:

Application	– The acquirer (being a shareholder of the target company) files an application proposing an arrangement or compromise between the target company and its shareholders and/or creditors.
Meeting of Members and/or Creditors	– Upon an application being made, the court may order a meeting to be held for each class of shareholders or creditors affected (as applicable).
Court Order on the Scheme	– If the meetings are held as ordered by the court, the court usually grants an order binding the scheme on all shareholders and creditors of the target company upon the satisfaction of the following: (1) for each class of creditors affected, a majority in number representing at least 75% in value of the class present and voting, in person or by proxy, at the meeting agree to the scheme; (2) for each class of shareholders affected: (a) shareholders representing at least 75% of the voting rights of the class of shareholders present and voting, in person or by proxy, at the meeting agree to the scheme; and (b) unless the court orders otherwise, a majority in number of the shareholders present and voting, in person or by proxy, at the meeting agree to the scheme.

[75] If the target company is a Hong Kong public company and/or listed company, additional requirements under the Listing Rules and Takeovers Code will apply. For instance:

– *Change of Control*. If the acquirer becomes, whether as a result of its share purchase or share subscription or the target company's share repurchase, a shareholder with more than 30% of the total voting power in the target company, the acquirer must launch a general offer to acquire the remaining shares from the other shareholders, unless the transaction falls within an exemption.[93]

- *Compulsory Acquisition*. If the acquirer seeks to 'squeeze out' minority shareholders by exercising its right of compulsory acquisition under statute, before the acquirer may exercise this right (assuming the statutory thresholds stipulated under the Companies Ordinance or (in the case of a listed company incorporated in an offshore jurisdiction) comparable thresholds, if any, stipulated under the laws of its home jurisdiction) are met, the acquirer's takeover offer must also satisfy the following additional requirements: (a) acceptances are received in respect of 90% of disinterested shares (i.e., shares other than those owned by the acquirer or persons acting in concert with it in the offer); and (b) the acceptances are received during the period of four months after the initial offer documents are posted.[94]
- *Scheme of Arrangement*. If the acquirer initiates a scheme of arrangement in the target company for the purpose of a takeover, before the acquirer may complete the takeover by means of the scheme (assuming the applicable statutory requirements and relevant court order, if any, are satisfied), in the meeting ordered for each class of shareholders affected, the scheme must also meet the following thresholds: (a) shareholders representing at least 75% of the voting rights of the disinterested shares (i.e., shares other than those owned by the acquirer or persons acting in concert with it) in that class present and voting, in person or by proxy, at the meeting vote for the scheme; and (b) the votes cast against the arrangement at the meeting does not exceed 10% of the total voting rights attached to all disinterested shares in that class.[95]
- *Delisting*. Before an acquirer may delist the shares of a listed company, (a) disinterested shareholders must adopt a resolution to approve the delisting, and the thresholds for its adoption are the same as in the scheme of arrangement of a public company as described above; and (b) the acquirer must be entitled to exercise, and is exercising its right of compulsory acquisition and the thresholds for its adoption are the same in the compulsory acquisition of a public company as described above.[96]

Acquisition of Hong Kong Businesses

[76] It is not uncommon to structure an acquisition as an 'asset transaction' with the expectation that liabilities not directly related to the assets will be excluded. In Hong Kong, this is possible if the required statutory procedures are completed before the closing of the transaction.

[93] Takeovers Code Rule 26.
[94] Takeovers Code Rule 2.11.
[95] Takeovers Code Rule 2.10.
[96] Takeovers Code Rule 2.2.

[77] Under the Transfer of Business (Protection of Creditors) Ordinance (the *Transfer of Business Ordinance*):[97]

- An acquirer is deemed to be liable for all the debts and obligations arising out of the carrying on of the target business by the seller, as well as the liability for tax charged or chargeable; but
- A creditor loses the right to make any claims against the acquirer for the seller's liability if: (a) the acquirer gives a notice of transfer not more than four months, but not less than one month, before the date of transfer and the transfer has been completed; (b) copies of the notice containing the required information are mailed to all of the creditors of the target business; and (c) the creditor does not initiate a proceeding against the acquirer within one month of the date of the notice.

[78] The failure to publish a notice does not impact the rights and obligations of the acquirer and the seller under the indemnities and warranties in a sale and purchase agreement. However, if any creditor institutes proceedings against the acquirer before the first anniversary of the transfer under the Transfer of Business Ordinance, the acquirer will become jointly and severally liable with the seller.

[79] To minimize the exposure of an acquirer in an assignment of debt and other liabilities, the acquirer should publish a notice to all of the creditors of the business upon the signing of the sale and purchase agreement and schedule the closing date of the acquisition to a date at least one month after the publication of the notice. The sale and purchase agreement typically requires a resolution to the acquirer's satisfaction if any proceeding is initiated during the period.

[80] To the extent the business involves a Hong Kong company or employees in Hong Kong, specific requirements also apply under the Employment Ordinance. *See* 'Employment Considerations'.

Acquisition of Hong Kong Licenses

[81] Many business operations, such as pharmacies, restaurants and education institutions, require special licenses under Hong Kong law. An acquirer may need to obtain new licences and permits due to ownership changes. Some license applications are straightforward, while others (including those triggered by acquisitions with no change in control) may not be possible under the law or may entail a lengthy and extensive process. The challenge sometimes lies in industry-specific regulations. Some licence applications could take months to amend, and existing licences could lapse in the meantime, especially when the acquisition results in a change of control occurs in the licensee.

[82] The issues could arise irrespective of whether the transaction is structured as a stock sale or asset sale. An example is the acquisition of a controlling stake in a television operator in Hong Kong. Although the acquisition is structured as a stock sale and the name of the licensee remains unchanged, the continued validity of the

[97] Sections 3 and 4, Transfer of Business (Protection of Creditors) Ordinance.

broadcasting license, likely one of the most valuable assets of the company, after the acquisition will be subject to regulatory approval.

[83] Generally licensing regulations in Hong Kong are more stringent in the following industries:

- *Broadcasting Companies*. Under the Broadcasting Ordinance, domestic free television programme service licensees and domestic pay television programme service licensees must be 'ordinarily resident' in Hong Kong.[98]

  An 'unqualified voting controller', which is defined to be a voting controller who is not an ordinary resident in Hong Kong, cannot, without the prior written consent of the Communications Authority, acquire interests in a domestic free television programme service licensee if the acquisition will result in its interests exceeding certain thresholds: 2%, 6% and 10%. This means a foreign acquirer cannot acquire meaningful interests in a domestic free television programme service business without prior regulatory approval.[99]

  Other than the restrictions summarized above, a 'disqualified person' must obtain approval from the Chief Executive-in-Council (meaning the Chief Executive has made the decision following advice from the Executive Council) to exercise control over more than 15% of voting shares of a licensed domestic free or pay television programme service provider. Disqualified persons are defined to include media operators or controllers in general.
- *Telecommunications Companies*. Under the Telecommunications Ordinance, the aggregate of the voting shares in a 'sound broadcasting licensee' controlled by non-ordinary residents in Hong Kong must not exceed 49%, and the licensee must be a Hong Kong incorporated company that is not a subsidiary of another corporation.[100]

  Pursuant to the Merger Rule under the Competition Ordinance, undertakings (as defined in paragraphs [100] and [101] below) holding a carrier licence within the meaning of the Telecommunications Ordinance must not carry out mergers having the effect of substantially lessening competition in Hong Kong.[101] Examples of merger include amalgamation of undertakings, acquisition of control of undertaking and acquisition of assets.
- *Authorized Institutions*. Hong Kong maintains a three-tier system for deposit-taking institutions: licensed banks, restricted licensed banks and deposit-taking companies. They are collectively known as authorized institutions. Under the Banking Ordinance, the prior approval of the Hong Kong Monetary. Authority is required before any person becomes a 'controller' (either alone or with associate(s) of 10% or more of the voting power) of an authorized institution incorporated in Hong Kong.[102]

[98] Section 8, Broadcasting Ordinance.

[99] Schedule 1, Broadcasting Ordinance.

[100] Section 13I, Telecommunications Ordinance.

[101] Schedule 7, Competition Ordinance.

[102] Section 70, Banking Ordinance.

- *Insurance Companies*. Insurance business is regulated in Hong Kong by the Insurance Ordinance (Cap. 41) and its subsidiary legislation. Section 8 of the Ordinance sets out the requirements on minimum amounts of paid-up share capital and solvency margin, fitness and properness of directors and controllers and adequacy of reinsurance arrangements in order to obtain the authorization to carry on insurance business in or from Hong Kong.
- *Securities Dealers and Investment Advisory Firms*. The Securities and Futures Ordinance identifies eleven types of regulated activities, including dealing or advising on securities or futures, asset management, foreign exchange trading, credit rating services, etc.[103] Individuals or companies must be registered with the Securities and Futures Commission to carry out these regulated activities. A person is required to apply for the approval of Securities and Futures Commission before such person (either alone or with associate(s)) acquires control of 10% or more of the voting power of a licensed corporation.[104]

Acquisition of Hong Kong Listed Shares

[84] Acquisition of a Hong Kong listed company usually falls into one of the following fact patterns:

- *Change of Control*. The acquirer's purchase of a significant number of shares gives it the right to direct the management and policies of the target company, but the business remains unchanged, and the target company remains a Hong Kong listed company.
- *Privatization*. The acquirer purchases all the shares held by shareholders in the target company (other than shares held by persons acting in concert with the acquirer) and causes the shares of the target company be delisted from the Hong Kong Stock Market.
- *Reverse Takeover*. The acquirer sells its business to a Hong Kong listed company with little or no business operations and/or negligible assets (generally known as a *shell company*) in exchange for a controlling stake in that company, with the practical effect of injecting the acquirer's business into a vehicle that is publicly traded on the Hong Kong Stock Market.

[85] An acquisition of share of listed companies can be structured in different ways. The following diagram classifies this kind of acquisition based on the objective and structure of the transaction.

[103] Schedule 5, Securities and Futures Ordinance.

[104] Section 131, Securities and Futures Ordinance.

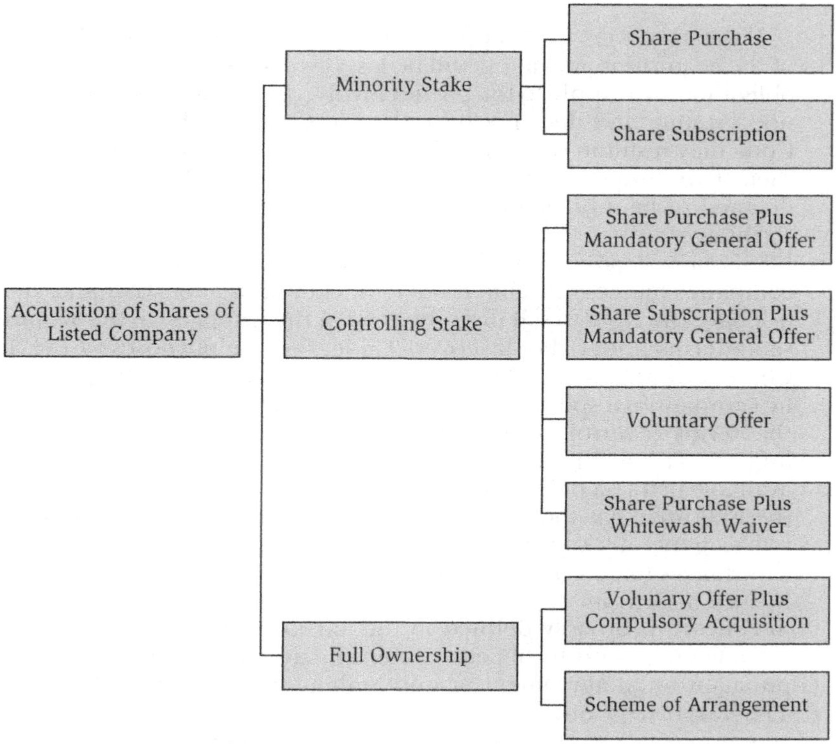

[86] Set forth below are preliminary considerations for an acquirer:

– *Whether the Takeovers Code Applies to the Acquisition*. Whether the Takeovers Code applies to the acquisition will depend on the nature of interest being acquired and the nature of the target company. Specifically:

(1) The Takeovers Code applies to 'offers for, and takeovers and mergers of', companies that are subject to the Takeovers Code. Examples of 'offers for, and takeovers and mergers of' companies include partial offers, offers by a parent company for shares in its subsidiary and certain other transactions where control of a company is to be obtained or consolidated. In contrast, offers for non-voting, non-equity securities are not 'offers for, and takeovers and mergers of' companies, unless the required non-voting, non-equity securities are convertible or acquired in connection with voting equities.

(2) The Takeovers Code covers 'public companies', 'companies with a primary listing of their equity securities in Hong Kong' and 'Real Estate Investment Trusts with a primary listing of their units in Hong Kong'. Hence, issuers with their stocks listed in Hong Kong, irrespective of their jurisdiction of incorporation, are within the scope of application of the Takeovers Code.

If the Takeovers Code applies, the structure, timing and substantive terms of the acquisition inevitably will be less flexible, and more onerous disclosure obligations will apply to the parties involved. Although the Takeovers Code is not a statute and does not have the force of law, a breach of the Takeovers Code may result in the imposition of a variety of sanctions by the Panel. Further, if the target company is in breach of the Takeovers Code, it will be deemed to be a breach of the company's listing agreement with the Stock Exchange.

- *Whether the Acquisition Will Trigger a Mandatory Offer*. When control of the company changes, all shareholders (including holders of equity derivatives) will have the right to sell their interests in the company to the acquirer on the same terms under the Takeovers Code. For the purposes of the Takeovers Code, 'control' means a holding of 30% or more of the voting rights of a public company, irrespective of whether that holding gives de facto control, and the terms 'control' and 'controlling shareholder' are construed accordingly.[105] This will have an impact on the amount of cash that must be made available before a definitive sale and purchase agreement is signed. Although the Executive has the power to waive the mandatory offer requirement, the waiver, generally known as a 'whitewash waiver', is only granted in limited circumstances (e.g., when target company is in financial distress).
- *Who are the 'Persons Acting in Concert' with the Acquirer*. The definition of 'acting in concert' is broadly defined in the Takeovers Code to cover persons who actively cooperate to obtain or consolidate control of the target company pursuant to an agreement or undertaking (whether formal or informal).[106] The Takeovers Code also specifies a list of persons who are presumed to be acting in concert unless the contrary is established.[107]

  In determining the interest held by the acquirer in the target company, the Takeovers Code consolidates the interests held by the acquirer with the interests held by 'persons acting in concert' with the acquirer (generally known as *concert parties*). It is important to identify all concert parties upfront because, among others, the outcome of that analysis will determine:
  (1) Whether the 30% threshold for the mandatory offer is triggered.
  (2) The minimum offer price.
  (3) The number of disinterested shares required to approve the privatization (if desired).
- *What is the Goal of the Acquisition*. Except with the consent of the Executive, all offers other than partial offers must be made conditional on the acquirer having received acceptances in respect of shares that, when aggregated with the shares already acquired or agreed to be acquired by the acquirer before or during the offer, will result in the acquirer and his concert parties holding more than 50% of the voting rights of the target company (the *standard 50% condition*).[108] This standard 50% condition is further accompanied by the following restrictions:

[105] Takeovers Code Definitions.
[106] *Ibid*.
[107] *Ibid*.
[108] Takeovers Code Rule 30.2.

(1) If the standard 50% condition is met, the acquirer may not make any offer or acquire shares of the target company at a price higher than the offer price for the six months following the completion of the offer.[109]
(2) If the standard 50% condition is not met and the acquirer chooses not to complete the offer, the acquirer may not make or announce any offer that will increase its shareholding to 30% or more of the voting rights of the target company for the twelve months following the completion of the offer.[110]
(3) If following the completion of the offer, the target company does not have the required minimum public float, the Stock Exchange may suspend trading of the target shares until appropriate action (such as a placing of shares) has been taken to restore an orderly market.[111]

Hence, the acquirer's interest in the target company will be subject to substantial economic uncertainty if the number of shares tendered in the offer is inconsistent with its objective in the acquisition.

- *How to Structure the Acquisition*. Although a voluntary acquisition may be structured in many different ways, some of which are discussed below, control must be acquired in good faith. All shareholders must be treated even-handedly, and all shareholders of the same class must be treated similarly.[112] The oppression of minority or non-controlling shareholders is unacceptable. Further, all shareholders of the target company are entitled to sufficient information, advice and time to reach an informed decision on an offer.[113]
- *Whether the Acquisition is a Hostile Takeover*. Hostile takeovers are rare in Hong Kong. The Takeovers Code prohibits the board of directors of a target company (*target board*) from taking any actions that are considered to be merely 'defensive' under other jurisdictions.

  Under the Takeovers Code, after a bona fide offer has been communicated to the target board, or when a target board has reason to believe that a bona fide offer might be imminent, the target board cannot, without the approval of shareholders in a general meeting, take any action in relation to the affairs of the target company that could effectively result in any bona fide offer being frustrated or in the shareholders being denied an opportunity to decide on its merits. Actions considered to be 'frustrating' and therefore are generally barred: (a) issuing shares, convertibles and options; (b) redeeming shares; (c) selling or acquiring assets of a material amount; and (d) entering into contracts outside of the ordinary course.[114]
- *Whether the Acquisition Constitutes a 'Reverse Takeover' under the Listing Rules*. The listing of equity securities on the Hong Kong Stock Market is subject to fairly stringent criteria under the Listing Rules, and the initial public offering (IPO) process can take nine to twelve months to complete. Hence, instead

[109] Takeovers Code Rule 31.3.
[110] Takeovers Code Rule 31.1.
[111] Main Board Listing Rules 8.08.
[112] Takeover Code General Principles.
[113] *Ibid*.
[114] Takeovers Code Rule 4.

of an IPO, an acquirer may desire to purchase a controlling stake in a shell company and, concurrently or shortly thereafter, cause the shell company to acquire the target business. An acquisition of this nature is labelled a *reverse takeover* under the Listing Rules. Not all target businesses in reverse takeovers fail to qualify for an initial listing on the Hong Kong Stock Market. Sometimes an acquirer prefers to bypass the traditional IPO route because a public offering of the target business is difficult due to lack of market interest, which could be linked to an industry downturn or the unrealistic valuation expectation of the business owner.

Reverse takeover is tightly regulated by the Stock Exchange. The Listing Rules define 'reverse takeover' to include the following events:[115]

(1) an acquisition or a series of acquisitions of assets constituting a very substantial acquisition (referred to generally as a '*VSA*') where there is or which will result in a change in control (as defined in the Takeovers Code) of the listed company (other than at the level of its subsidiaries); or
(2) acquisition(s) of assets from a person or a group of persons or any of his/their associates (*see* 'Acquisition of Assets Held by Hong Kong-Listed Companies' in this section below for definitions of the term 'associate' under the Listing Rules) pursuant to an agreement, arrangement or understanding entered into by the listed company within twenty-four months of such person or group of persons gaining control (as defined in the Takeovers Code) of the listed company (other than at the level of its subsidiaries), where such gaining of control had not been regarded as a reverse takeover, which individually or together constitute(s) a VSA.

In reviewing potential reverse takeover transactions, the Stock Exchange may go beyond the above-mentioned bright-line tests and look more closely at the intention of the transaction. In determining whether an acquisition constitutes a reverse takeover, the Stock Exchange may consider, among other factors:

(1) whether the acquisition would result in a change of the principal business of the listed company;
(2) the size of the acquisition relative to the listed company;
(3) whether the target company would be able to satisfy the minimum new listing requirements; and
(4) whether the target company would be suitable for listing.[116]

The Stock Exchange may also require a proposed acquisition be aggregated with other acquisitions completed by the listed company within twenty-four months and classify the series of acquisitions as a reverse takeover.[117]

[115] Main Board Listing Rule 14.06 (6).
[116] Main Board Listing Rule 8.04 and HKEx guidance Letter HKEx-GL78-14.
[117] Main Board Listing Rule 14.06(6)(b).

Acquisition of Assets Held by Hong Kong Listed Companies

[87] This section discusses the acquisition of assets from Hong Kong listed companies, including the purchase of subsidiaries, business divisions and/or other assets held by such companies. The main regulations applicable are the Listing Rules and the Securities and Futures Ordinance. For simplicity, we will limit our discussion to the purchase of assets from a Hong Kong listed company by an unlisted acquirer. Very similar regulations apply when the transaction involves a sale of assets to a Hong Kong listed company, except that this type of acquisitions could raise 'reverse takeover' concerns.

[88] Set forth below are some preliminary considerations for an acquisition of this nature:

- *How Significance is Determined.* The Listing Rules contain comprehensive rules governing the acquisition or disposal of assets by a listed company ('subject assets'). These requirements are set forth in Chapter 14 of the Listing Rules, in which transactions are classified by the percentage ratios resulting from the following 'size tests'.[118]

Assets ratio:	$\dfrac{\text{Subject assets}}{\text{Total assets of the company}}$
Profits ratio:	$\dfrac{\text{Profits attributable to the subject assets of the transaction}}{\text{Total profits of the company}}$
Revenue ratio:	$\dfrac{\text{Revenue attributable to the subject assets}}{\text{Revenue of the company}}$
Consideration ratio:	$\dfrac{\text{Consideration}}{\text{Total market capitalization of the company}}$
Equity capital ratio:	$\dfrac{\text{Number of shares of the company to be issued as consideration}}{\text{Total number of issued shares of the company immediately before the transaction}}$

[118] Main Board Listing Rule 14.07.

Where any calculations of the percentage ratios produce an anomalous result or are inappropriate to the activities of the company, the Stock Exchange may disregard the above and considers alternative meaningful calculation methods or test submitted by the company on a case-by-case basis.

- *How Significant is the Transaction under the Grading Scale.* The Listing Rules classify the significance of an acquisition based on the outcome of the five 'size tests' described above.

  The following list summarizes the classification of transactions based on their percentage ratios computed under the 'size tests':[119]
- *What are the Disclosure Requirements.* Depending on the percentage ratios resulting from the five 'size tests', different announcement, disclosure and shareholder approval requirements apply. A transaction in which any of these requirements is triggered is a 'notifiable transaction'. 'Notifiable transactions' are primarily governed by Chapter 14 of the Listing Rules.

[89] The following table summarizes the notification, publication and shareholder approval requirements for each type of transaction:[120]

Share transaction (acquisition of assets excluding cash):	Where all percentage ratios are less than 5%
Disclosable transaction:	Where any of the percentage ratios is 5% or more but less than 25%
Major transaction (acquisition):	Where any of the percentage ratios is 25% or more but less than 100%
Very substantial acquisition of assets (VSA):	Where any of the percentage ratios is 100% or more

	Notification to Exchange	*Publication of Announcement*	*Circular to Shareholders*	*Shareholder Approval*	*Accountants Report*
Share transaction	Yes	Yes	No	No	No
Disclosable transaction	Yes	Yes	No	No	No

[119] Main Board Listing Rule 14.08.

[120] Main Board Listing Rule 14.33.

	Notification to Exchange	*Publication of Announcement*	*Circular to Shareholders*	*Shareholder Approval*	*Accountants Report*
Major transaction	Yes	Yes	Yes	Yes	Yes
Very substantial acquisition	Yes	Yes	Yes	Yes	Yes
Reverse takeover	Yes	Yes	Yes	Yes	Yes

[90]

– *Whether the Acquisition involves a 'Connected Person'*. In addition to assessing the classification of the acquisition under the 'notifiable transaction' requirements as described above, the parties should also determine whether a transaction is a connected transaction under the Listing Rules. If any contractual party in the acquisition is a 'connected person' of the listed company, the transaction is likely a 'connected transaction'. 'Connected transactions' are primarily governed by Chapter 14A of the Listing Rules.

The term 'connected persons' is broadly defined under the Listing Rules to provide safeguards against directors, chief executives and substantial shareholders (or their 'associates') taking advantage of their positions when the listed company enters into transactions with them. Generally, 'connected persons' include:[121]

(1) Directors, chief executive, 'substantial shareholders' (i.e., holders of 10% or more of the voting power at any general meeting) of the listed company and any person who was a director of the listed company in the past twelve months (referred to in this article collectively as *core affiliates*);
(2) 'Associates' of the foregoing persons; and
(3) Non-wholly owned subsidiaries of the listed company where connected persons of the listed issuer (other than at the level of its subsidiaries) have 10% or more of the voting power ('affiliated entities') and subsidiaries of such affiliated entities.[122]

However, if a subsidiary of a listed company is a 'connected person' only because it is a subsidiary of an affiliated entity, transactions between these subsidiaries do not fall within the definition of 'connected transactions'.

In the context of connected transactions, 'associates' are widely defined and include:

(1) In the case of a core affiliate who is a natural person: (a) his or her immediate family members (i.e., spouse and children), the trustees of any

[121] Main Board Listing Rule 14A.07.
[122] Main Board Listing Rule 14A.16.

trusts in which the core affiliate and his or her immediate family members are beneficiaries; and entities in which the core affiliate, the trustees of his or her family trusts and his or her immediate family members have 30% or more of the voting power or the ability to control a majority of the board of directors and the subsidiaries of such entities;[123] (b) his or her expanded family members (i.e., person cohabiting as a spouse, parents and siblings) and entities in which his or her expanded family members have 50% or more of the voting power or the ability to control a majority of the board of directors;[124] and (c) to the extent deemed appropriate by the Stock Exchange, his or her further expanded family members (i.e., in-laws, grandparents, grandchildren, nephews and nieces) and entities in which his or her further expanded family members have 50% or more of the voting power or the ability to control a majority of the board of directors.[125]

(2) In the case of a core affiliate that is a corporate entity: (a) any entity that is its holding company or a subsidiary or a fellow subsidiary of its holding company (each, a *group member*); (b) the trustee of any trust in which the core affiliate is a beneficiary (a *corporate interest trustee*); and (c) any entity in which the core affiliate, together with its group members and corporate interest trustees, have 30% or more of the voting power or the ability to control a majority of the board of directors.[126]

(3) Any person or entity with whom a core affiliate has entered into, or proposes to enter into any arrangement with respect to the acquisition that is in the opinion of the Stock Exchange, should be considered a connected person.[127]

Only a narrow category of connected transactions are exempt from the disclosure, reporting and shareholder approval requirements. One main exemption is a connected transaction on normal commercial terms where all of the percentage ratios (other than the profits ratio) are (x) less than 0.1%; or (y) less than 1% and the transaction is connected only because it involves a person who is a connected person of the Hong Kong listed company by virtue of its relationship with the company's subsidiary(ies); or (z) less than 5% and the total consideration is less than HKD3 m.[128]

A connected transaction on normal commercial terms where each or all of the percentage ratios (other than the profits ratio) are (x) less than 5% or (y) less than 25% and the total consideration is less than HKD10 m are exempt from reporting and independent shareholders' approval.[129]

The shareholder approval requirement will increase uncertainty in the successful completion of the acquisition because any shareholder with a

[123] Main Board Listing Rule 14A.12.

[124] *Ibid.*

[125] Main Board Listing Rule 14A.21.

[126] Main Board Listing Rule 14A.13.

[127] Main Board Listing Rule 14A.20.

[128] Main Board Listing Rule 14A.76(1).

[129] Main Board Listing Rule 14A.76(2).

material interest in the acquisition and its associates must abstain from voting.

- *Whether the Target Assets involve a Mineral Company.* A transaction involving the acquisition of mineral or petroleum assets and a Hong Kong listed company is subject to additional requirements under Chapter 18 of the Listing Rules. Among others, the requirement of a competent person's report may impact the timing of the acquisition.[130]

Regulations Applicable to Business Controllers

Duties of Directors

[91] Directors' duties can be classified into internal and external standards.

[92] Internal standards are those set forth in the company's constituent documents, internal guidelines issued by the company and directors' service contracts with the company. External standards are the legal requirements made applicable to the directors through the company, including the laws of the company's jurisdiction of incorporation, the rules of the stock exchange on which the shares of the company are listed and, in some cases, the governing law of the transaction. A director needs to satisfy both the internal and external standards.

[93] In most cases, the Hong Kong legal requirements are not the only external standards applicable to a director, and not all Hong Kong standards are applicable. By way of example, when a Cayman Islands company listed on the Hong Kong Stock Exchange conducts a share placement in the United States, and one of the placees is affiliated with its chairman, the chairman needs to consider his fiduciary duties under the laws of the Cayman Islands as opposed to Hong Kong common law; he also needs to consider his disclosure duties as a controlling person of the company under the US securities laws.

[130] Main Board Listing Rule 18.09(2).

[94] The following diagram summarizes the various external standards:

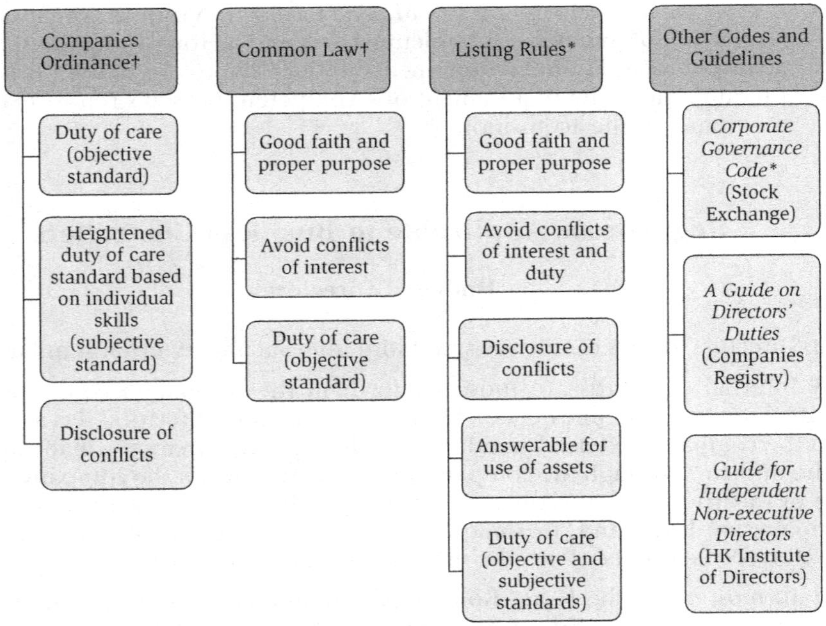

* Hong Kong listed companies only.
† Hong Kong incorporated companies only.

– *Common Law.* Under the common law, directors' duties to a Hong Kong company consist of two types: duties of care, diligence and skill; and fiduciary duties. Duties of care, diligence and skill are derived from tort principles and require directors to satisfy certain minimum standards when performing their roles and exercising their powers. Fiduciary duties are derived from equitable principles and require directors to act solely in the best interest of the company. Common law does not distinguish among executive directors, non-executive directors and independent non-executive directors.

  Under case law that continues to have binding authority in Hong Kong, the standard of care, skill and diligence is a subjective one: a director is only required to exercise such skill as is reasonably expected from a person with similar knowledge and experience. This standard has been superseded by the Companies Ordinance as described below.

– *Companies Ordinance.* On directors' duties of care, diligence and skill, the Companies Ordinance prescribes a standard that diverges from the Hong Kong common law but is consistent with the modern judicial interpretation in many other common law jurisdictions. This standard contains an objective and a subjective component. A director is required to exercise the reasonable care, skill and diligence that would be exercised by a reasonably diligent person in such capacity. This objective standard will be adjusted upward if a director possesses additional skills and experience, in which case the director will be measured against a person with such general knowledge, skill and experience.

On directors' fiduciary duties, a director of a Hong Kong company must disclose to the board of directors if he has an interest in a material contract or arrangement proposed to be entered into by the company and the extent and nature of such interest. A director should not borrow from the company, nor should the company provide other kinds of financing support such as acting as a guarantor or providing assets as security for his personal loan, unless the financing support falls within the narrow circumstances prescribed in the statute.

- *Listing Rules.* Of particular importance to directors of Hong Kong listed companies are the Listing Rules. Although the Listing Rules do not have the force of law, a breach of the Listing Rules could result in the forced retirement of the director from the company, the imposition of other sanctions on the director and the company, as well as a cancellation or suspension of the company's listing.

  Directors' duties under the Listing Rules can be broadly divided into three categories. The first category is analogous to the fiduciary duties under common law: to act honestly and in good faith in the interests of the company as a whole, act for a proper purpose, and avoid actual and potential conflicts of interest and duties. The second category is analogous to the fiduciary duties under the Companies Ordinance: to disclose fully and fairly his or her interests in contracts with the company and to seek disinterested shareholder approval before taking part in loans and similar transactions with the company. The third category is analogous to the duties of skill, care and diligence under the Companies Ordinance, plus an emphasis that the performance of such duties cannot be excused by delegation.
- *Other Codes and Guidelines.* For directors of Hong Kong listed companies, the Corporate Governance Code is also relevant to the extent it sets forth standards expected of directors in their handling of the listed company's affairs, including acquisitions. The Guidance for Boards and Directors provides guidance in specific areas and provides practical advice to board and directors and sets out expectations placed on directors in some cases.

  All directors, including those of a private company, are expected to be familiar with the general duties outlined in 'A Guide on Directors' Duties' issued by the Companies Registry, as well as the 'Guidelines for Directors' and the 'Guide for Independent Non-executive Directors' published by the Hong Kong Institute of Directors.

  Although the principles set forth in these codes and guidelines are not mandatory, they will be taken into account by the courts in assessing whether a director has met the requisite standard of skill and care in the discharge of his or her duties. In the context of directors' conflicts, these guidelines require a director not to accept any benefit from a third party, if such benefit is conferred because of the powers he or she has as a director or by way of reward for any exercise of his or her powers as a director.

Duties of Responsible Persons

[95] 'Responsible persons' is a statutory term under the Companies Ordinance and includes a company's officers (including its directors, company secretary and manager) and shadow directors (including an officer or shadow director of a corporate officer or corporate shadow director). Under the ordinance, responsible persons of a Hong Kong or non-Hong Kong company will be criminally liable if the company is in breach of certain ordinance provisions and such persons authorize or permit, or participate in the contravention of the failure.[131] These include the failure to report changes in material particulars of the company[132] and to comply with the statutory requirements when the company reduces its share capital[133] or provides financial assistance to a third party in an acquisition of its own shares.[134]

Disclosure Duties of Shareholders

[96] Substantial shareholders (defined in the Securities and Futures Ordinance as persons interested in more than 10% of the issued share capital) of a listed company are required to disclose, through public filings, their ownership interests in the listed company. The disclosure requirements are set forth under Part XV of the Securities and Futures Ordinance, and the key concepts are summarized as follows:

- *Notifiable Interests*. An 'interest' in the issued share capital is defined to include direct interests in voting shares; interests in unissued voting shares through ownership of equity derivatives; indirect interests of voting shares or equity derivatives through intermediate holding companies, discretionary trusts, concert party agreements and immediate family members; and contingent interests such as a security interest.[135] Hence, interests in options, subscription warrants and convertible bonds (among others) are potentially disclosable, but (unless the investor is also a director of the company) interests in non-voting preferred stock and debentures are not.
- *Initial and Subsequent Reporting*. A disclosure obligation generally arises when a person acquires an interest of 5% or more in the issued share capital of the company.[136] Following the initial reporting, any changes in the nature or amount of such interests (apart from those falling within the exemptions) must also be reported.
- *Reporting of Short Positions*. A person with a notifiable interest in the company is also obligated to disclose any short position exceeding 1% or more of the issued share capital of the same company.[137]

---

[131] Section 3, Companies Ordinance.

[132] Sections 645(6), 652(3), 88(6), 107(6), and 658(5), Companies Ordinance.

[133] Section 212, Companies Ordinance.

[134] Section 275, Companies Ordinance.

[135] Sections 322 and 323, Securities and Futures Ordinance.

[136] Sections 311(3) and 315, Securities and Futures Ordinance.

[137] Section 315(2), Securities and Futures Ordinance.

- *Exemption for De Minimis Changes*. Following the initial reporting, any subsequent changes in the amount of interest or short position in the relevant shares are exempt from reporting if they fall within a *de minimis* range.[138] There are detailed rules providing for whether a fraction of a percentage change is a *de minimis* change.
- *Exemption for Securities Lending and Borrowing*. Changes in the nature of an interest of a substantial shareholder (but not a director or chief executive) arising on the lending and return of shares to an 'approved lending agent' using a specified form of agreement are exempt from reporting.[139]
- *Exemption for Qualified Securities Interest*. The creation of the security interest in favour of a 'qualified lender' will not result in a change in the nature of the holder's interest in those shares.[140] Similarly, a 'qualified lender' will not have a notifiable interest if it holds the shares 'by way of security only' in a transaction entered into in the ordinary course of his business.[141]
- *Directors and Chief Executives*. The disclosure requirements are more stringent if the person is also a director and/or chief executive of the company and/or its 'associated companies', which is widely defined to include holding companies and subsidiaries of the listed company, other subsidiaries of the listed company's holding companies and any entities in which the listed company has a 20% shareholding interest.[142] Among others, such a person is required to disclose interests in any shares (not just voting shares) or debentures of the company and its 'associated companies'. Further, the *de minimis* exemption and lending shares exemption are not available.

[97] The disclosure filing must be made with the Stock Exchange and the listed company at the same time or one immediately following the other. Subject to limited exceptions, the time period for notifications of certain relevant events is ten business days (in the case of an initial notification) and three business days (in the case of the other 'relevant events' defined in section 308 of the Securities and Futures Ordinance).

ANTITRUST/COMPETITION ISSUES

Competition Ordinance

[98] The Competition Ordinance was enacted on 14 June 2012 as the first cross-sector competition law in Hong Kong. The legislation came into full effect on 14 December 2015.

[138] Section 313, Securities and Futures Ordinance.

[139] Section 3, Securities and Futures (Disclosure of Intrerest-Securites Borrowing and Lending) Rules.

[140] Section 313(13), Securities and Futures Ordinance.

[141] Section 323(6), Securities and Futures Ordinance.

[142] Section 308, Securities and Futures Ordinance.

[99] Provisions in the Competition Ordinance governing the formation of the Competition Commission came into force on 18 January 2013. The Competition Commission is a statutory body with investigation and enforcement powers. Provisions in the Competition Ordinance governing the formation of the Competition Tribunal came into force on 1 August 2013. The Competition Tribunal is a court with the power to impose sanctions, hear appeals against decision of the Competition Commission, and adjudicate private actions seeking damages from statutory violations of the ordinance.

[100] The Competition Commission has, to date, issued two policy documents, six guidelines and four guidance notes. These set out how the Competition Commission intends to interpret and give effect to the legislation and exercise its investigation and enforcement functions.[143]

[101] One fundamental concept in the Competition Ordinance is the term 'undertaking'. An 'undertaking' is 'any entity, regardless of its legal status or the way it is financed, engaged in economic activity and includes a natural person engaged in economic activity'.[144] The definition is intended to limit the proscribed activities under the ordinance to persons that engage in economic activities only. For instance, a non-governmental organization publishing market research and issue guidance on minimum wage levels is not an 'undertaking'.

[102] Another fundamental concept is whether two or more undertakings constitute a single economic unit.[145] Generally, a holding company and its subsidiaries are of the same economic unit, while joint venture partners are of different economic units. The rationale is that entities within the same group should be permitted to make their internal arrangements to increase their market competitiveness, but market players should not be permitted to agree on arrangements that would have an anti-competitive effect.

Conduct Prohibited by the Ordinance

[103] The Competition Ordinance sets out three key rules, known respectively as the First Conduct Rule, the Second Conduct Rule and the Merger Rule. Underscoring the extraterritorial reach of the Competition Ordinance, the competition rules apply regardless of whether the conduct occurs, or whether any of the undertakings are located, outside Hong Kong:

[104] The First Conduct Rule prohibits undertakings from participating in agreements, concerted practices or decisions of trade associations that have the object or

[143] Competition Commission website, https://www.compcomm.hk/en/legislation_guidance/guidance/guidance.html, https://www.compcomm.hk/en/legislation_guidance/guidance/other/other_guidance.html, https://www.compcomm.hk/en/legislation_guidance/policy_doc/policy_doc.html, accessed on 27 Dec. 2018.

[144] Section 2, Competition Ordinance.

[145] Paragraphs 2.6–2.10 of Communications Authority and Competition Commission, joint guideline on the First Conduct Rule.

effect of harming competition in Hong Kong.[146] The First Conduct Rule is mostly concerned with preventing cartel arrangements among competitors, and the Competition Commission has publicly stated that cartels will be the primary target of its investigations and enforcement efforts. Such cartel arrangements are described in the Competition Ordinance as 'serious anti-competitive conduct' and includes price fixing, market sharing, output restriction/limitation and bid-rigging.

[105] The Second Conduct Rule prohibits undertakings that have substantial market power in a market from abusing that power by engaging in conduct that has the object or effect of harming competition in Hong Kong.[147] There are no limitations on what constitutes 'abuse' under the Competition Ordinance, but the guideline gives five examples: predatory pricing, anti-competitive tying and bundling, margin squeeze, refusals to deal and exclusive dealing. There is no universal test for determining whether an undertaking has a substantial degree of market power. Rather, the Competition Commission will assess market power based on various factors, including market share, market concentration, countervailing buyer power, barriers to entry or expansion and any characteristics that are specific to the relevant market. The relevant market is assessed by reference to the product market and geographic market. While the Competition Commission will have regard to previous cases when defining the relevant market, the guideline states that the definition will depend on the specific facts of the case and the Competition Commission is not bound by previous decisions.

[106] The Merger Rule prohibits an undertaking from carrying out a merger that has, or is likely to have, the effect of substantially lessening competition in Hong Kong. At present, the Merger Rule is only of limited application and applies only when one of the undertakings participating in the proposed merger holds a carrier licence within the meaning of the Telecommunications Ordinance.[148] While it is anticipated that the ambit of the Merger Rule will be extended across all business sectors, there is as yet no confirmed timeframe for the implementation.

[107] The Competition Ordinance contains a number of exclusions and exemptions.[149] By way of example:

- *Economic efficiency*: The First Conduct Rule does not apply to agreements that enhance overall economic efficiency. The undertaking will need to show, among other things, that the agreement contributes to improving production or distribution, or promotes technical or economic progress and that the arrangement benefits consumers or at least causes no prejudice to consumers in the market. Where an undertaking uses identical or substantially similar agreements to conduct business, it may apply to the Competition Commission for a block exemption order.
- *Legal requirement:* The First Conduct Rule and the Second Conduct Rule do not apply if the agreement or conduct in question is made or carried out in

[146] Section 6, Competition Ordinance.
[147] Section 21, Competition Ordinance.
[148] Schedule 7, Competition Ordinance.
[149] Schedule 1, Competition Ordinance.

compliance with a legal requirement. However, the fact that anti-competitive behaviour may have been accepted or even encouraged in the past is insufficient. To minimize the risk of non-compliance, an undertaking should carefully assess whether it comes squarely within the exclusion.

- *Agreements of lesser significance (and do not involve serious anti-competitive conduct)*: The First Conduct Rule does not apply if the combined turnover of the undertakings in relation to the arrangement does not exceed HKD200 m.
- *Conduct of lesser significance*: The Second Conduct Rule does not apply to conduct engaged in by an undertaking if its turnover during the preceding calendar or financial year does not exceed HKD40 m.
- *Statutory bodies*: The competition rules do not apply to a statutory body unless it is specifically brought within the scope of the rules by a regulation made by the Chief Executive. This exclusion does not extend to an entity that is owned or controlled by a statutory body unless the entity is also a statutory body.

Consequences of Anti-competitive Conduct

[108] The Competition Commission is equipped with an array of tools and remedies aimed at encouraging compliance with the competition rules and to punish offenders when necessary. If the Competition Commission considers that an undertaking has contravened a competition rule, it may:

- Issue a warning notice to the undertaking, giving the undertaking a warning period within which to cease the contravening conduct.[150]
- Issue an infringement notice to the undertaking, offering to not bring proceedings in the Competition Tribunal on the condition that the undertaking makes a commitment to comply.[151]
- Accept a commitment from the undertaking to take, or refrain from taking, certain actions to address the concerns about a possible contravention.[152]
- Request the Competition Tribunal to impose fines and other orders on the undertaking.[153]

[109] The Competition Tribunal is empowered to impose fines on any undertaking that contravenes the competition rules. The maximum fine for each breach of the competition rules is 10% of the turnover of the undertaking concerned for each year in which the contravention occurred, capped at three years.[154] Turnover is defined as the total gross revenues of an undertaking obtained in Hong Kong. Additionally, the Competition Tribunal may make any orders that it thinks fit, including:

- Disqualifying a person from being a director or otherwise involved in the promotion, formation and management of the company for up to five years.

[150] Section 82, Competition Ordinance.
[151] Section 67, Competition Ordinance.
[152] Section 60, Competition Ordinance.
[153] Section 92, Competition Ordinance.
[154] Section 93, Competition Ordinance.

- Issuing mandatory and prohibition orders, as well as injunctive relief.
- Requiring the payment of damages to aggrieved parties.
- Declaring an agreement to be void or voidable, requiring the modification or termination of an agreement and prohibiting a person from giving effect to an agreement.[155]

[110] Following a finding of contravention by the Competition Commission or the Competition Tribunal, private parties may seek damages by instituting proceedings before the Competition Tribunal.[156]

Leniency Policy

[111] The Competition Commission considers cartel conduct to be a serious and harmful threat. Because it is usually organized and implemented in secret, the existence of a cartel can be difficult to detect and the gathering and analysis of evidence is a costly and time-consuming exercise.

[112] In view of these challenges, the Competition Commission intends to use leniency as a tool to encourage an undertaking that is willing to end its involvement in cartel conduct to come forward and cooperate. In essence, provided that it satisfies all of the requirements for leniency, the first member of a cartel to report the cartel conduct will not be subject to any fines or other orders.[157] Under the leniency agreement, the undertaking will be required to provide its full cooperation to the Competition Commission, for example, by providing all relevant information (which is not legally privileged) and testifying against the other cartel members.

[113] A leniency agreement, however, only provides immunity against the imposition of fines and other orders by the Competition Tribunal. It will not provide any protection against follow-on private actions brought by aggrieved parties who have suffered damage as a consequence of the cartel's conduct.

TAXATION ASPECTS

General

[114] Hong Kong has a relatively simple tax regime. The major types of taxes are:

- *Profits Tax*. Profits tax is levied on individuals, partnerships and entities carrying on a trade, profession or business in Hong Kong in respect of assessable income arising in or derived from Hong Kong.
- *Salaries Tax*. Salaries tax is levied on individuals in respect of income arising in or derived from Hong Kong from any office, employment or pension.

[155] Schedule 3, Competition Ordinance.

[156] Section 110, Competition Ordinance.

[157] Section 80, Competition Ordinance.

- *Property Tax*. Property tax is levied on individuals owning buildings or land in Hong Kong in respect of rental income derived from such assets. Companies receiving rental income may elect to pay profits tax instead of property tax on such income.
- *Stamp Duties*. Stamp duties are levied on transactions involving immovable properties in Hong Kong and Hong Kong stocks. Stamp duties consist mainly of the ad valorem stamp duties chargeable on the sale of immovable properties, leasing of immovable properties and transfer of Hong Kong stocks. In addition to the ad valorem stamp duty, special stamp duty and buyer stamp duty are also chargeable on the sale of residential properties under certain situations.

Taxes Relevant to Mergers and Acquisitions

[115] A planned industry-specific M&Atax structure may achieve and improve tax efficiency for the enlarged group post mergers and acquisitions, taking into account tax, commercial and financial perspectives and ideally capturing upside potentials and downside risks. While a professional tax adviser is more suited to advise on tax structuring, we set out below nonetheless a general overview of the more significant types of taxes in the context of mergers and acquisitions: profits tax on business operations and stamp duties on corporate transactions.

Taxes on Business Operations

[116] The following summarizes the key principles of taxation applicable to the operation of a business in Hong Kong:

- *Profits Tax*.

  Profits tax is imposed on a person 'carrying on a trade, profession or business' in respect of his or her 'Hong Kong-sourced' 'assessable profits':[158]

  (1) The tax applies to all forms of businesses, regardless of whether it is a company registered in Hong Kong, sole proprietorship, partnership (limited or unlimited) or branch of a foreign entity. The current profits tax rate for incorporated businesses is 16.5% while the rate for unincorporated businesses is 15%. However, from the year of assessment 2018/2019 onwards, one enterprise among connected entities can elect for its first HKD2 m assessable profits be taxed 8.25% (for incorporated businesses) or 7.5% (for unincorporated businesses).

  (2) The threshold for 'carrying on a trade, profession or business' in Hong Kong is low. Foreign companies, however, may avoid double taxation if they are based in a country with a tax treaty with Hong Kong. Hong Kong has concluded comprehensive double taxation agreements with forty jurisdictions.

[158] Section 14, Inland Revenue Ordinance.

(3) The determination of the source of profits is set out in the Inland Revenue Department guidelines. Generally, if the main activities leading to the profits occur in Hong Kong, the profits are 'Hong Kong-sourced', although apportionment of profits between two or more jurisdictions is possible.

- *Property Tax.* Property tax applies to the 'net assessable value' of 'immovable property' in Hong Kong. However, the tax does not apply if a property owner is a corporation and elects to be subject to profits tax on income received from the property.
- *Value-Added Tax.* There are no value-added, goods and services or turnover taxes in Hong Kong.
- *Withholding Tax.* Withholding tax is only imposed on 'non-residents' in respect of 'royalties', consignment sales and payments to entertainers or sportsmen, etc.
- *Group Companies.* There is no tax consolidation or group relief regime. Profits and losses arising in different companies of the same group are managed separately.

Taxes on Corporate Transactions

[117] The following summarizes the key principles of taxation applicable to an acquisition of asset in Hong Kong:

- Stamp duties apply to agreements for sale of 'immovable property' located in Hong Kong, conveyances of 'immovable property' located in Hong Kong, transfers of 'Hong Kong stock', leases of 'immovable property' located in Hong Kong and issuances of 'Hong Kong bearer instrument'. Relevant rules are as follows:

  (1) *Transfer of Hong Kong stock.* Ad valorem stamp duty at the rate of 0.2% applies on the transfer of Hong Kong stock based on the value of the shares transferred or the purchase price paid, whichever is greater.[159] 'Hong Kong stock' is defined to include shares in Hong Kong incorporated companies and shares in companies incorporated outside Hong Kong with their issued shares recorded on a register maintained in Hong Kong.[160] The stamp duty is payable by the seller and the buyer equally and must be paid before the transfer of shares can be registered in the books of the target company and within the time periods specified in the Stamp Duty Ordinance.

  (2) *Transfer of non-residential property.* Ad valorem stamp duty at progressive rates of up to 8.5% applies on the transfer of non-residential property located in Hong Kong based on the value of property or the purchase price paid, whichever is greater.[161] The duty is payable on the date of agreement for sale and all parties executing the instrument are liable for

[159] Schedule 1, Stamp Duty Ordinance.
[160] Section 2, Stamp Duty Ordinance.
[161] Schedule 1, Stamp Duty Ordinance.

the duty. A formal conveyance executed in conformity with the stamped agreement for sale will only attract an additional amount of stamp duty at the fixed rate of HKD100.

(3) *Transfer of residential property*. There are three types of stamp duties potentially payable on the transfer of residential property in Hong Kong. All three types of stamp duties are calculated based on the value of property or the purchase price paid, whichever is greater. All three types of stamp duties are payable on the date of agreement for sale and all parties executing the instrument are liable for the duties:[162]
   (a) Ad valorem stamp duty of a flat rate of 15% of the consideration or value of the property (whichever is the higher) applies to instruments of residential property executed on or after 5 November 2016. Residential properties acquired by a Hong Kong permanent resident who does not own any other residential property in Hong Kong at the time of acquisition are subject to ad valorem stamp duty at progressive rates of up to 4.25%.
   (b) Special stamp duty at varying rates of up to 20% applies when two conditions are met: (x) the property was acquired by or transferred to the property owner on or after 27 October 2012; and (y) the property was disposed of or transferred by the property owner within thirty-six months from the date of acquisition.
   (c) Buyer's stamp duty at the rate of 15% applies to any person (including a Hong Kong corporation) who acquires a residential property located in Hong Kong on or after 27 October 2012. Purchase by a Hong Kong permanent resident is exempted from buyer's stamp duty.

(4) *Intragroup transfer exemption*. The intragroup transfer exemption from stamp duties (provided certain conditions are fulfilled) is commonly relied upon by companies with the same parent. This exemption applies to a transfer of Hong Kong stock or immovable property located in Hong Kong.[163]

This exemption is available when a transaction party is directly or indirectly the beneficial owner of not less than 90% of the other transaction party, or a third-party corporation is the beneficial owner of not less than 90% of the issued share capital of each transaction party. Under such circumstances, stamp duties are not payable when the transaction meets the following conditions: (a) the consideration or any part thereof is not provided by a party other than an associated corporation; (b) the consideration or any part thereof is not received by an unassociated corporation and relevant interest being transferred was not previously conveyed, transferred, purchased or sold directly or indirectly by an unassociated person; and (c) the transferor

[162] Schedule 1, Stamp Duty Ordinance.
[163] Section 45, Stamp Duty Ordinance.

and transferee do not cease to be associated as a result of a change in shareholding of the transferee within two years after the date of execution of the instrument.

The following taxes are not imposed in Hong Kong:

(1) Capital Gains Tax. There is no capital gains tax in Hong Kong. Whether gains on the disposal of assets, including shares, are 'capital' in nature is a question of fact. No single test is determinative. An important factor considered by Hong Kong courts is whether there is an intention to trade.
(2) *Dividend Tax*. Dividends, whether received in Hong Kong or overseas, are not taxable.
(3) *Capital Duty*. Capital duty was abolished in Hong Kong in June 2012. No taxes are payable in issuance of shares.

Taxation Matters in Mergers and Acquisitions

[118] Acquirers should consider the following if the target company is a Hong Kong company or the target assets are in Hong Kong:

- *Stamp Duties Payable*. Due to the large difference between the rate of the stamp duty applicable to a transfer of stock and that applicable to a transfer of real property, an asset sale may attract significantly higher stamp duty cost if the target assets consist of real properties.
- *Transaction Costs*. Transaction costs such as legal fees and due diligence costs should be prima facie deductible if the acquirer (e.g., a private equity fund) derives assessable profits from their investment activities. In contrast, transaction costs incurred in connection with the acquisition of a capital asset held for investment purposes are not deductible.
- *Finance Costs*. Interest expense is deductible only if such expense is incurred for the purpose of producing assessable profits and meets one of the specified conditions. Generally, interest on debt incurred for the purpose of an asset acquisition is a deductible expense if the debt is provided by a financial institution or any other Hong Kong-based entity. In contrast, interest on debt incurred for the purpose of acquiring shares that are held for long-term share investment is not. This is largely grounded on the principle that dividends received from the target company are not taxable.
- *Clawback of Intragroup Exemption Previously Recognized*. An acquirer in a stock acquisition should pay special attention to whether the target company made any claims for intragroup exemption from stamp duties in the past two years. If the target company ceases to remain a member of the group within two years as a result of a change in its beneficial ownership, the stamp duties previously exempted will become payable on the date on which the target company ceases to be a group member.
- *Profits Tax Payable by Seller*. Although Hong Kong does not levy any capital gain tax on the disposition of shares in a Hong Kong company, there might

be a profits tax implication if the profit is deemed as profit derived in Hong Kong by a person carrying on a trade, profession or business. For example, if the selling shareholder holds the target shares on revenue account, the gain from the sale of the target shares could potentially be subject to Hong Kong profits tax as trading profits, unless the shareholder has no presence in Hong Kong and does not carry on any activities in Hong Kong (either directly or through an agent).

[119] The following should be considered in determining the tax value of the target business:

- *Tax Basis of Target Assets*. In Hong Kong, the step-up of tax basis is not applicable in a stock acquisition. The target company will retain the same tax basis for its assets regardless of the price paid for its shares. In contrast, an asset acquisition may allow the acquirer to reset the tax basis of the assets.
- In an asset acquisition, the seller and the acquirer should agree on an apportionment of the purchase price between the different types of assets being transferred.
- *Tax Losses in Target Company*. Tax losses may generally be carried forward indefinitely to offset against a company's future taxable profits unless the sole or dominant purpose of the acquisition is to acquire the tax losses. Note that the target company's tax losses will not be available to related companies because there is no tax consolidation. Also, tax losses cannot be transferred in an asset acquisition.
- *Capex on Plant and Machinery*. The acquirer may claim allowances for qualified capital expenditures incurred on the acquisition of plant and machinery items (at 60% of the acquisition cost). The acquirer may also deduct annual allowances at rates prescribed by the Inland Revenue Department on the reducing value of the asset. The rates are 10%, 20% or 30% according to the nature of the asset. Items qualifying for the same rate of annual allowance are grouped in one pool. Prescribed assets, such as computer systems and manufacturing machinery, subject to limitations, can qualify for a 100% write off for tax purposes in the year of acquisition.
- *Capex on Industrial Buildings*. Special allowances are given in respect of capital expenditures incurred on the construction of industrial buildings and structures used in certain trades, such as transport, dock, water and electricity undertakings, the manufacture, processing or storage of goods and trades carried on in mills and factories and in farming. An initial allowance of 20% of such capital expenditures will be given in the year of expenditure and an annual allowance of 4% of the capital expenditures will be given until all the capital expenditures are written off. When the asset is disposed of, a balancing allowance or balancing charge is made based on the difference between the disposal price (limited to original cost) and the written-down value on disposal.
- *Goodwill and Intangible Assets*. There is no depreciation or deduction available for goodwill acquired in the transaction. Tax deduction, however, is generally available to the acquirer on the acquisition of specified intellectual property rights for use in the production of chargeable profits. A 100% deduction for

the expenditures incurred on patent rights or rights to any know-how will be allowed in the year of purchase. A 20% deduction on the expenditures incurred on copyrights, registered designs or registered trademarks will be allowed for five consecutive years starting from the year of purchase. However, such deduction is not allowed where the transfer was made between associated parties.

EMPLOYMENT CONSIDERATIONS

General

[120] Employment matters in Hong Kong are mainly governed by the Employment Ordinance. The ordinance covers the payment of wages and the termination of employment contracts and affords employees who have worked under 'continuous contracts' various statutory benefits and protections. An employee who has been employed continuously by the same employer for four weeks or more, with at least eighteen hours worked in each week, is regarded as being employed under a 'continuous contract'.[164]

[121] Generally, an employment contract may be terminated by the employer or the employee through giving the other party notice or wages in lieu of notice. Special considerations, however, have to be given in cases involving union membership, sick leave, maternity leave, whistle-blowing or industrial accidents as there are restrictions on whether an employee can be terminated under those circumstances.

Termination of Employees

[122] An acquirer may want to restructure the target business, resulting in the termination of certain positions in the company. The following matters have to be considered when terminating employment contracts:

- *Minimum Notice Period/Payment in lieu of Notice*. During probation, a contract of employment can be terminated (x) without notice within the first month of probation and (y) after the first month of probation, by giving not less than seven days' notice or wages in lieu of notice.[165] Where there is no probation or after probation has been completed, not less than one month's notice is required unless there is agreement as to the length of notice, in which case the terms of such agreement will prevail, provided that not less than seven days' notice is given.
- *Termination Payment*. The type and amount of payment payable to an employee on the termination of employment or expiry of the contract

[164] Schedule 1, Employment Ordinance.
[165] Section 6, Employment Ordinance.

depend on a number of factors, such as the length of service, the terms of the employment contract and the reasons for the termination. Notably, two types of payments required by the Employment Ordinance may be applicable:

(1) *Severance Payment.* An employee who has been employed under a continuous contract for twenty-four months or more and is dismissed by reason of redundancy is entitled to a severance payment. The amount of severance payment is two-thirds of the employee's last full month's wages or two-thirds of HKD22 500, whichever is less, for each year of service.[166] The maximum severance payment payable is HKD390 000.[167] The amount of any gratuity or retirement scheme payment to the employee, based on length of service, is deductible from the amount of severance payment entitlement. In the case of a retirement scheme payment, only the employer's contributions (and interest thereon) may be deducted.[168]

(2) *Long Service Payment.* An employee is entitled to a long service payment on termination of employment by the employer if he/she (x) has been employed under a continuous contract for five years or more and (y) is dismissed for any reason other than redundancy or misconduct.[169] An employee who has been paid a severance payment will not be entitled to a long service payment. The calculation of long service payment is the same as severance payment and is also subject to the same maximum amounts as stated above.[170]

– *Unreasonable and Wrongful Dismissal.* As in many other jurisdictions, an employer will have litigation risks if it terminates an employee other than for a valid reason as specified in the Employment Ordinance or if the dismissal is in contravention of other applicable law, such as the anti-discrimination ordinances. In addition, if the terms of the employment contract are varied without the employee's consent and the employment contract does not contain an express term which allows for such a variation, this will constitute constructive dismissal.[171]

Employment Matters in Mergers and Acquisitions

[123] Employment issues are generally not problematic in a stock acquisition. An acquirer would largely depend on the due diligence conducted prior to the transaction to identify issues with respect to labour and employment contracts in place, such as 'change of control' payments in an executive contract. These issues usually can be managed by contractual provisions in the share purchase agreement.

166 Section 31G, Employment Ordinance.
167 Section 31G and Schedule 7, Employment Ordinance.
168 Section 31I, Employment Ordinance.
169 Sections 31R and 31S, Employment Ordinance.
170 Section 31V, Employment Ordinance.
171 Section 32A, Employment Ordinance.

[124] If the acquisition is in the form of a transfer of business (i.e., where asset and goodwill of an enterprise are sold or transferred on a going concern basis), Hong Kong law provides that the contracts of the employees, including written or implied oral agreements, do not automatically transfer to the acquirer. Accordingly, when the acquirer acquires the business, all existing employment contracts with employees will be deemed to have been terminated, and termination payment may become due and payable.

[125] The acquirer of a business, however, can minimize its liability of termination payments by following the following procedures:

- notice is given to the employee offering employment not less than seven days before the date of the employees' transfer;
- the offer of employment to the employees is on terms that are either identical to those under the employees' existing employment contract or constitute a written offer of suitable employment on terms no less favourable to the employees than those under which they were previously employed;
- employment is renewed on or before the date of termination of the employment contract with the former owner; and
- the acquirer agrees to recognize the employees' previous service for the purpose of calculating severance payment or other benefits in the future.

[126] Provided that the above requirements are fulfilled, the acquirer will not be required to make any statutory severance payments when an employee unreasonably refuses an offer on these terms. However, if the employee elects to terminate his or her contract and has been under continuous employment for five years or more as of the termination date, he or she will still be entitled to the long service payment.[172]

ACCOUNTING TREATMENT

General

[127] Hong Kong companies are required to prepare their accounts under the Hong Kong Financial Reporting Standards (*HKFRS*). The HKFRS sets out recognition, measurement, presentation and disclosure requirements for the reporting of transactions and events that are important in general purpose financial statements. The application of HKFRSs, with additional disclosure when necessary, is presumed to result in financial statements that give a 'true and fair view' of the financial position, financial performance and cash flows of a company.

[128] The HKFRS consists of accounting standards, financial reporting standards and interpretations. Each standard relates to a specific topic such as presentation of financial statements, inventories, statement of cash flows and income taxes. One of the main principles of Hong Kong accounting standards (*HKAS*) is that an entity

[172] Section 31R, Employment Ordinance.

prepares its financial statements, except for cash flow information, using the accrual basis of accounting.

Accounting Treatment for Business Combinations

[129] The financial reporting by an entity when it undertakes an acquisition is governed by HKFRS 3, Under HKFRS 3, a 'business combination' is defined as a transaction or other event in which an acquirer obtains control of one or more businesses and therefore, the term covers different types of M&Ain their ordinary meanings. In particular, HKFRS 3 specifies that all business combinations should be accounted for by applying the acquisition method unless it is a combination involving entities or businesses under common control or the acquiree is a subsidiary of an investment entity which is required to be measured at fair value through profit or loss. Formations of a joint arrangement in the financial statements of the joint arrangement itself or the acquisition of an asset or a group of assets that does not constitute a business are not 'business combinations' under HKFRS 3.

[130] Under the acquisition method, the acquirer recognizes the target company's identifiable assets, liabilities and contingent liabilities, non-controlling interests in the target company and goodwill or a gain from a bargain purchase as at the acquisition date. These items are measured, with some exceptions, at their fair values. Some assets and liabilities are required to be recognized or measured in accordance with other standards rather than at fair value. These include assets and liabilities falling within the scope of *HKAS* 12 (Income Taxes), HKAS 19 (Employee Benefits), HKFRS 2 (Share-based Payment) and HKFRS 5 (Non-current Assets Held for Sale and Discontinued Operations):

- *Fair Value*. Fair value is the price that would be received to sell an asset or paid to transfer a liability in an orderly transaction between market participants at the measurement date. HKFRS 13 defines fair value, provides guidance on how to measure fair value under HKFRS and requires information about those fair value measurements to be disclosed.
- *Acquisition Date*. Acquisition date is defined as the date on which the acquirer effectively obtains control of the target company. An investor controls an investee when it is exposed, or has rights, to variable returns from its involvement with the investee and has the ability to affect those returns through its power over the investee; therefore, it is not necessary for a transaction to be closed or finalized at law before the acquirer obtains control. All pertinent facts and circumstances surrounding a business combination are considered in assessing when the acquirer has obtained control.

Treatment of Key Items

[131] The following summarizes the treatment to be accorded to the key items in a business combination:

- *Consideration.* The acquirer measures the cost of a business combination as the aggregate of the fair values of assets given, liabilities incurred or assumed and equity instruments issued by the acquirer, in exchange for control of the target company. The fair values of these items are measured as at the acquisition date.
- *Transaction Costs.* These are costs such as professional fees paid to accountants, legal advisers, valuers and other consultants to effect the business combination. They do not include general administrative costs, such as the costs of maintaining an acquisitions department. Such costs shall be accounted for as expenses in the periods in which the costs are incurred and the services are received. The costs to issue debt or equity securities are recognized in accordance with HKAS 32 and HKFRS 9.
- *Identifiable Assets and Liabilities of Target Company.* The identifiable assets and liabilities that are recognized in accordance with the requirements set forth in HKFRS 3 include all of the target company's assets and liabilities that the acquirer purchases or assumes, including all of its financial assets and financial liabilities. The more common items encountered include the following:
  (1) *Restructuring costs.* Restructuring costs can be recognized as new liabilities and typically include payments that the target company is contractually required to make to its employees in the event that it is acquired in a business combination. Such payments constitute a present obligation of the target company that is regarded as a contingent liability until it becomes probable that a business combination will take place. The contractual obligation is then recognized as a liability by the target company in accordance with HKAS 37 when a business combination becomes probable and the liability can be measured reliably. Therefore, when the business combination is effected, that liability of the target company is recognized by the acquirer as part of allocating the cost of the combination.

  In contrast, the target company's restructuring plan whose execution is conditional upon it being acquired in a business combination is not, immediately before the business combination, a present obligation of the target company. Nor is it a contingent liability of the acquirer immediately before the combination because it is not a possible obligation arising from a past event whose existence will be confirmed only by the occurrence or non-occurrence of one or more uncertain future events not wholly within the control of the target company. Therefore, an acquirer cannot recognize a liability for such restructuring plans as part of allocating the cost of the combination.

  (2) *Tax losses.* Certain assets not previously recognized in the target company's financial statements can be recognized as new assets. For instance, a tax benefit arising from the target company's tax losses that was not recognized by the target company before the business combination qualifies for recognition as an identifiable asset if it is probable that the acquirer will have future taxable profits against which the unrecognized tax benefit can be applied.

(3) *Non-controlling interests.* Components of non-controlling interests in the target company can be recognized at either fair value or the proportionate share in the recognized amounts of the target company's identifiable net assets, and such value should be assessed by reference to the acquisition date.

– *Goodwill and Intangible Assets of the Target Company.* Goodwill and intangible assets are acquired in a business combination at cost less any accumulated impairment losses:

(1) *Goodwill.* Goodwill is defined under HKFRS as future economic benefits arising from assets that are not capable of being individually identified and separately recognized. Goodwill acquired in a business combination represents a payment made by the acquirer in anticipation of future economic benefits from assets that are not capable of being individually identified and separately recognized. It is measured as the excess of (x) the aggregate of the consideration transferred and the amount of any non-controlling interest in the target company over (y) the net of the acquisition-date amounts of the identifiable assets acquired and the liabilities assumed. If the acquirer has made a gain from a bargain purchase, that gain is recognized in profit or loss.

(2) *Intangible Assets.* Intangible asset is defined under HKFRS as an identifiable non-monetary asset without physical substance. HKAS 38 provides guidance on determining whether the fair value of an intangible asset acquired in a business combination can be measured reliably. In accordance with HKAS 38, an asset meets the identifiability criterion in the definition of an intangible asset only if it: (a) is separable (i.e., capable of being separated or divided from the entity and sold, transferred, licensed, rented or exchanged, either individually or together with a related contract, identifiable asset or liability); or (b) arises from contractual or other legal rights, regardless of whether those rights are transferable or separable from the entity or from other rights and obligations.

[132] HKAS 36 sets forth the procedures that a company must take to ensure that its assets (including goodwill and intangible assets) are carried at no more than their recoverable amount. An asset is carried at more than its recoverable amount if its carrying amount exceeds the amount to be recovered through use or sale of the asset. Carrying amount is the amount at which an asset is recognized after deducting any accumulated depreciation (amortization) and accumulated impairment losses thereon. Recoverable amount is the higher of (x) fair value less costs of disposal and (y) value in use.

[133] If the carrying amount of an asset exceeds its recoverable amount, the asset is described as impaired, and HKAS 36 requires the company to recognize an impairment loss. An impairment loss is the amount by which the carrying amount of an asset exceeds its recoverable amount.

[134] At each reporting date, an assessment must be made to determine whether there is any indication that an asset may be impaired. If any such indication exists, the recoverable amount of the asset must be determined. Further, goodwill and intangible assets with an indefinite useful life must be tested for impairment annually irrespective of whether there is any indication that such assets may be impaired, or more frequently if events or changes in circumstances indicate that they might be impaired, in accordance with HKAS 36.

RECENT DEVELOPMENTS

Backdoor Listings

[135] Hong Kong regulators are increasingly critical of the large number of 'backdoor listings' on the Hong Kong Stock Market. A backdoor listing in Hong Kong typically involves a sale of the business to be listed to a listed company with minimal business operations (commonly labelled as a *shell company*), resulting in the seller of the business acquiring control of the listed company through its receipt of new shares or convertible bonds of the listed company as consideration for the sale. From the regulators' perspective, 'backdoor listings' are undesirable because in many cases the business is of substandard quality, the stock price of the shell company shows signs of market manipulation, and the controlling persons and public float of the shell company are dubious. From the market's perspective, 'backdoor listings' are a practical, market-driven solution for small to medium companies in China to continue their growth, given the long list of companies awaiting regulatory approval for their initial public offerings in China and the challenge to complete their initial public offering in Hong Kong at satisfactory valuation.

[136] The reverse takeover provisions in the Listing Rules were enacted to discourage backdoor listings. As the regulators continue to tighten the rules, business operators and market players continue to modify their transaction structures in response. For example, parties may have the acquirer (i.e., the business owner desiring to have its business listed) make cash investments into the shell company through a subscription of new shares or convertible securities. These large-scale fundraisings usually result in the business owner acquiring a controlling stake in the shell company and the cash would then be invested into the business through different contractual arrangements, marginalizing the shell company's original business, assets and results of operations.

[137] The Stock Exchange is increasingly sceptical of large-scale fundraising with one or more of the following characteristics:

- the size of the proposed fundraising is very significant to the listed company and unrelated to the needs of its existing principal business;
- the new investors acquire control of the listed company and change its board of directors;
- the cash proceeds are used for a new business substantially larger than the listed company's existing business.

[138] The Stock Exchange's concern is that these activities are, in substance, backdoor listings of businesses that do not meet the requirements for a new listing.

[139] The Stock Exchange has been acting more aggressively against backdoor listings, having taken a high-profile position publicly on this subject and rejected backdoor listings more frequently. It is expected that the Stock Exchange will continue to issue stricter rules to regulate backdoor listings. At the same time, the regulators' position on backdoor listings made 'shell companies' more valuable in the market. Some market players conducted small initial public offerings for single-line businesses with minimal non-current assets and offered them as 'shell companies' for small to medium companies in China after the expiration of the one year lock-up period for a change of control transaction. In June 2018, the Stock Exchange proposed a number of new rules and to tighten the continuing listing criteria to address concerns about backdoor listings and shell activities, including a ban that prohibits listed companies from selling major assets or business within thirty-six months after a change of control transaction. The Stock Exchange also published a guidance letter on listed issuer's suitability for continued listing in the same month, citing examples of circumstances where the Stock Exchange may raise concerns on the issuer's suitability for continued listing. For example, the Stock Exchange may have concern if the issuer, instead of genuinely operating a business of substance, seems only carrying on its business for the purpose of maintaining a listing status.

[140] Due to the Stock Exchange's sensitivity on backdoor listings, smaller listed companies may find it increasingly difficult to complete major acquisitions or dispositions with real economic substance. This is because the Stock Exchange's prior approval is needed before a listed company may release an announcement for a very substantial acquisition or disposition or convene a shareholders meeting to approve the transaction.

VIE Structures

[141] Some Hong Kong listed companies have a variable interest entity (generally known as *VIE*) structure. The structure is commonly found in companies operating in certain industries such as the media and telecommunications sectors and the medical sector in China where foreign ownership is prohibited. Under a VIE structure, the Hong Kong listed company enters into long term and extendable contractual arrangements, pursuant to which the Hong Kong listed company, through one or more wholly owned PRC subsidiaries, effectively controls and consolidates the financial position and operating results of the PRC operating entities owned by PRC nationals. The Hong Kong listed company recognizes and receives substantially all economic benefits of the business and operation of the PRC operating entities and their operating results are reflected in the consolidated financial statements of the Hong Kong listed company under applicable accounting principles.

[142] In an arbitration award rendered in 2011, a PRC arbitration tribunal considered a contractual dispute arising from a VIE structure. The tribunal was of the view that the VIE arrangement had violated PRC regulations prohibiting foreign investments in restricted sectors and hence was invalid. However, as an arbitral award is the result of a private dispute resolution and has no judicial standing, it only serves as mere guidance as to how a court might approach similar matters. Legal risks and uncertainties related to VIE structures remain.

[143] In a court ruling rendered in 2012, the PRC Supreme Court considered the use of an entrustment structure in a restricted industry. Although the court did not directly challenge the legality of the VIE structure, it nevertheless ruled that where agreements were entered into with the clear intent of circumventing China's restrictions on foreign investments in certain restricted industries and the contractual parties intentionally breach PRC laws and regulations, such agreements are invalid and unenforceable.

[144] In Guidance Letter 77-14, which was first published in May 2014 and last updated in April 2018, the Stock Exchange limits the conditions in which listed companies may acquire or set up new businesses through VIE structures. The Guidance Letter follows the principles in Listing Decision 43-3, which was first issued in 2005 and last updated in April 2018, the Stock Exchange indicated that applicants with VIE structures will be assessed based on the following general principles:

(1) *General.* Listing of such applicants will be assessed on a case-by-case basis, if (x) the Stock Exchange is satisfied as to the reasons for the use of the structured contracts; and (y) the applicant complies with requirements of the listing decision.
(2) *Restricted Businesses.* The Stock Exchange only accepts the use of VIE structures in restricted businesses with foreign ownership restrictions; applicants using VIE structures in non-restricted businesses will be referred to the Listing Committee of the Stock Exchange for consideration.
(3) *Regulatory Compliance.* Applicants must demonstrate that they have, upon legal advice, reasonably assessed the requirements under all applicable rules other than the foreign ownership restrictions, and have taken all reasonable steps to comply with these rules. They must obtain appropriate regulatory assurance from the relevant regulatory authorities; in the absence of such regulatory assurance, the applicant's PRC legal counsel must issue a statement to the effect that all possible actions or steps have been taken to enable it to reach its legal conclusion.
(4) *Undertaking to Restructure.* Applicants must agree to unwind the VIE structure as soon as the law allows the business to be operated without them; shareholders of the PRC operating entity must undertake to return to the applicant any consideration received when the VIE structure is unwound.
(5) *Control and Ownership.* Shareholders of the PRC operating entity must agree to grant powers of attorney to the directors of the applicant so that they can exercise shareholders rights on their behalf. Applicants must have, under appropriate dispute resolution clauses, meaningful recourse against assets held by the PRC operating entity.
(6) *Legal Opinion.* Where the relevant laws and regulations specifically disallow foreign investors from using any agreements or contractual arrangements to gain control of or operate a foreign restricted business, applicants' PRC legal counsel opinion must include a statement confirming that the VIE

structure does not constitute a breach of PRC laws and will not be deemed invalid or ineffective under PRC laws or regulations.

As a result of the Stock Exchange's position on VIE structures, businesses that are eligible for a listing on Nasdaq or the New York Stock Exchange (*NYSE*) may not qualify for an initial listing in Hong Kong. Similarly, if a party desires to sell a business with a VIE structure to a Hong Kong listed company, such party should check if the business would meet the requirements under the Guidance Letter.

[145] In January 2015, the Ministry of Commerce issued a consultation draft of the new PRC foreign investment law. It is proposed that the draft new law will replace the three existing pieces of PRC legislations governing foreign investment activities in the country. The proposed law, if fully implemented, will very likely eliminate VIE structure explicitly, while it is still uncertain whether existing VIE structures may be preserved. On 23 December 2018, the draft new law was presented to the Standing Committee of the National People's Congress for deliberation, which is considered a relatively late stage in the legislative process in the PRC. In view of the proposed new law's potential impact on VIE structure, the Stock Exchange encouraged applicants with VIE structures to seek its guidance at the earliest possible opportunity.

Made in the USA
Monee, IL
13 September 2026

62974260R00057